# FUNDAMENTALS OF *Music Appreciation*

# FUNDAMENTALS OF *Music Appreciation*

BY

HUMMEL FISHBURN
*The Pennsylvania State University*

REVISED EDITION

DAVID McKAY COMPANY, INC.
NEW YORK

FUNDAMENTALS OF MUSIC APPRECIATION



FIRST EDITION JULY 1955
REPRINTED NOVEMBER 1955
NOVEMBER 1956
JULY 1959
DECEMBER 1960
SEPTEMBER 1962
REVISED EDITION, JANUARY 1964

LIBRARY OF CONGRESS CATALOG CARD NUMBER: 55–8883

Printed in the United States of America

THIS

BOOK IS DEDICATED

TO

*Rebecca C. Fishburn*

WHO KEPT URGING HER HUSBAND

TO STOP PROCRASTINATING AND

TO GET A MANUSCRIPT

FINALLY READY FOR

PUBLICATION

# Preface

THE FIRST edition of this book was published in 1955; it was written to fill a need in our colleges and universities for a general nontechnical course based on the admitted purpose of acquainting the student with certain information about music that would be useful to him in his post-collegiate life as he might listen to concerts or to the musical offerings of radio and television. If there was a need for such a book in 1955, and we believe there was, the need seems to be growing rather than diminishing, for with the added emphasis on scientific studies in the realm of education that has come with the conquest of space, the humanities and arts and social sciences tend to be minimized in the curriculum, in spite of brave words to the contrary on the part of some of our most-quoted educational writers.

And since 1955 other needs for such a book as this that were not recognized at the time have become evident. Not only colleges and universities, but junior colleges, community colleges, high schools offering an emphasis in music, and more recently adult education programs have found this to be a text suitable for their educational goals.

We readily admit that a certain percentage of college-level students has garnered a considerable amount of information about music from the listening point of view as well as from the performance angle, either through private study or by taking advantage of the musical offerings of preparatory and high schools. It is equally true that in many of our secondary schools the music instructor is so busy perfecting the performing groups (which unfortunately often serves as the basis of judgment of his ability as a teacher by the public) that the "other 80 per cent" of the student body is musically neglected. Institutions training music teachers for the public schools are aware of this problem and are seeking to rectify it in their courses of study; nevertheless, the neglect does exist, as has been shown by studies made by Elmer C. Wareham of the music faculty of the Pennsylvania State University.

There are numerous books on the market designed to give the student an insight into music from the appreciative basis. Many of these are excellent, and fill a need. But they fill a need in the further education of students who have a knowledge of musical theory and terminology and notation gained prior to their use. We use such a text in an advanced course in musical literature, but find that we cannot presuppose this previous musical knowledge in dealing with a large percentage of college students, for it simply isn't there in many cases. This is the basis for this text, in which we have attempted to use only that part of musical nomenclature and theory that we consider to be absolutely necessary in training for selective listening.

The book is divided into several parts. First, there is a logical approach to the fundamentals of music in which an attempt is made to make the reader conversant with those component parts of music that appear in every worth-while composition. Then comes a chronological survey of the subject. Here there is no attempt to produce a history of music, but rather a cause-and-effect basis is used to treat the more significant occurrences through the course of musical history that might lead the listener to understand better the music produced in any given period or country. Within this historic approach are mentioned those composers who seem outstanding in their art product: but here again there is no attempt to go into the minutiae of their lives, but simply to give them their rightful places in the over-all musical development. A third section of the book acts as a corollary to the other sections in that it suggests recorded material to be used in connection with the study, for since music is an aural art listening is the important phase of the study, and the written text is simply provided to help the student to a better understanding of the music he hears. In this revision some new recordings have been listed, particularly in the vocal field, so that the listener will be led to the great singers of the present generation as well as some of the great names from an earlier age.

While minor revisions of the text have been made for clarification, the only other major revision is in the final chapter where there has been an attempt to include a survey of some of the most important changes in contemporary music. In the over-all history of music ten years is only a fleeting fraction of time, but in the span of modern music ten years is a large segment of the total: much could happen in this time—and much has happened.

Our philosophy in first writing a text of this type can be shown by the following incident. Some years ago an intercollegiate boxing champion from Penn State was a member of our class; at the beginning of the course he professed to know nothing about music—and he was right in this assumption. After completing the semester course, and after the grades had been recorded so that there could be no possibility of "apple-polishing" on his part, he was asked to give a frank opinion of the course. His reply was revealing: "You know," he said, "every day I train for an hour or two, and then I like to relax for a while before dinner by listening to my radio. I always used to twist the dials around until I got a dance orchestra or a crooner, but now if it happens to be one of those symphony or opera things you told us about I can leave it there and listen to it—and I like it."

# Acknowledgments

THE AUTHOR is indebted to many persons for their helpful suggestions during the writing of this book, and wishes to give special mention to the following individuals and groups:

Those members of the staff of Music and Music Education at the Pennsylvania State University who carried the load so that time could be available for writing and research.

Professor G. William Henninger for his suggestions relative to the sections on harmony and form.

Professor Theodore K. Karhan for his aid in the listings for stringed instruments.

Elmer C. Wareham for his general help in the whole project.

Mrs. Barbara Fahrney for typing the manuscript.

H. Ross Fishburn for his counsel concerning the whole subject of jazz.

Peter C. Fishburn for making all drawings, charts, and diagrams.

Professor Andrew W. Case for clarification of certain phases of the section on Early Christian music.

Rabbi Benjamin M. Kahn for information concerning Hebrew music.

Angelo D. Vespa for the use of his record library.

And the thousands of students in the course in Music 5 at the Pennsylvania State University who went through the experimental stages of the general music appreciation course during which the present approach was evolved.

H.F.

# *Contents*

## *Part I. Introduction*



## *Part II. The Five Fundamentals of Music*

## *Part III. The Highlights of Musical History*

PART I

# Introduction

CHAPTER I

# The Teaching of Music Appreciation

TO UNDERSTAND the philosophy behind the writing of this book it is first necessary to realize that the appreciation of music, or of any other art, cannot be taught, for appreciation of an art takes into consideration not only the subject matter but also the individual reaction of the perceiver, which in the case of music is obviously the listener. "To appreciate" is variously defined as "to esteem adequately, perceive distinctly; to raise in value; to estimate; to be keenly sensible of or sensitive to." An appreciation, then, is a sensitivity to the art in the make-up of the individual. It stems from the individual himself and is his reaction to the form and color of a painting, the flow of words in poetry, the tune and rhythm and harmony of a musical composition performed for his listening.

There are a number of factors in the make-up of any person that may affect his sense of appreciation. One factor may be the national background of his family, which would be at least partially responsible for those people who prefer arias from the Italian operas, or polkas, or the music of the *kozatski*. A second factor might be the geographical area in which a person is brought up, which would help to account for the popularity of hillbilly music and cowboy songs in some sections of the country. The fact that the radio or television stations on which a given segment of the population is dependent for its listening might offer a diet of musical presentations predominantly hillbilly, or jazz in any of its various ramifications, or even a classical fare might be another factor in the musical likes and dislikes of an individual, which is to say, in his appreciation. Perhaps through training he has been shown certain musical features that give him a chance to absorb the most out of the music in question; this would be still another factor. All of these (and this is not a complete list) combined in the make-up of an individual in varying degrees of emphasis will tend to give him a personal response of enjoyment to various kinds of music: he may prefer a single type of music, or be equally fond of several types. He may even have favorite specific compositions. But because of the factors involved his favorites and yours are likely to be quite different.

This preference of certain individuals for certain types of music, or for certain specific compositions within these types, is all to the good, for if it were not so music would be a pretty stereotyped affair. If we all liked the same things a variety in musical composition would be unnecessary. Composers would all write for the masses and there would therefore be a definite limitation on genius and on much that seems fine and worthwhile to at least some segment of the population.

One of the factors that has been mentioned as a possible means of help toward the appreciation of music is the matter of training. You may enjoy (and therefore appreciate) a football game, or a wrestling meet, or a chess match. But it is doubtful if you would enjoy watching any of these contests of skill to the fullest extent if you were ignorant of the plays, or the holds, or the moves used in outwitting the opposition. Would you rather see a football game or a cricket match? It is true that a person can go to a football game on a brisk autumn afternoon and thoroughly enjoy the experience because of the crowds and the more than incidental music, but he will not get a full measure of appreciation of the event until he knows the relative merits of the systems involved and can take into consideration the performance of the twenty-one men who are not carrying the ball at the moment as well as that of the ball-carrier. Training in an understanding of the fundamentals of good football is an essential for true appreciation of the game, whether that training be self-taught or through a course of instruction.

And so it is with music. There are many people who, through the medium of their own listening and observation, have discovered enough about the subject to have a good appreciation of fine music and fine musical performances. But this seems to be the long way around, and in this age of specialization and with the many things we must attend to in order to get an education and make a living it seems a more sensible approach to have some of these fundamentals pointed out to us so that we may understand more rapidly, and with this understanding better appreciate music as one of the great arts.

This takes us back to the original statement in this chapter: that the appreciation of any art cannot be taught. But by pointing out some of the important essentials of the music itself it is possible to give the listener a better chance to learn to appreciate it much sooner than he might do otherwise.

# The Physical Basis of Sound

THE PHYSICIST is interested in sound as one of the many natural phenomena of the world. But sound as such is a large field; one small portion of that field is musical sound. The branch of the science of physics that treats of the phenomena and laws of sound is known as acoustics; one subdivision of acoustics considers music. Even here there are further subdivisions, for the acoustics expert is interested not only in the physical production of a musical tone, but also in the transmission of the tone and the reception of the tone by the listener. The subject is too large and too technical for us to go into in much detail, but some basic facts that will give us a picture of the musical tone as produced, and the various factors of the tone as they are interpreted through our hearing apparatus, can be presented. In the matter of the interpretation we also call upon the findings of the psychologist, who has an interest in the interpretation of sensations by the ear and by our other sensory receptors.

When a sound is produced, it is due to an action that causes sound waves to be sent forth. A number of factors are present in the original impetus, such as the materials involved, the method of using these materials in the initial impulse, and the force used. Each of these plays a part in the resultant size and shape and speed of the sound wave.

The physicist has developed a very useful instrument known as the oscilloscope which gives us an actual picture of the sound waves produced by an impact. To keep this discussion from being too technical, suppose we imagine a small screen similar to the picture tube of a television set. As sounds are produced into a microphone, they will be reproduced electrically as visual images on the screen, enabling us to study them by sight. As tones are produced by a violin or a trumpet or the voice, the variations in the resultant sound pictures are easily seen. All of these vibrations will have certain things in common, but they will vary in the number of ups and downs that will show on the screen, in the size from top to bottom of these ups and downs, and in the actual shape of each separate but similar unit. The physicist calls these the *frequency,* and *amplitude,* and the *complexity* of the particular tone being heard and thus being pictorially reproduced.

The *frequency* is measured by the number of complete vibrations that occur in a time period of one second. When these varying frequencies reach the ear, we hear the differences in degrees of highness or lowness of the tone: the greater the frequency, the higher the tone. What we term *pitch* is, therefore, our psychological interpretation of the frequencies we hear. The average human ear is able to hear tones with frequencies ranging from about 20 to approximately 20,000 per second. This range covers the whole gamut of musical sound, from the tones produced by the largest organ pipes to those made as harmonics on the violin. Obviously, the musician is only interested in those sounds that can be heard by human beings, but the physicist also studies and utilizes the sounds above this range in the field of ultrasonics.

The *amplitude,* or size of the sound waves, is received by us as the loudness or softness of the tone produced. The physicist uses decibels as his measuring device for amplitude, and while this is a rather technical thing to understand, we can think of musical tones as having a range from the just audible to those that approach causing actual pain to the listener because of their loudness. The physical amplitude is translated in our reception as the psychological *volume* of tone.

The *complexity* of the shape of the vibrations depends upon the number and relative strength of the overtones that are produced by the sound medium in addition to the fundamental or basic tone set up by the vibrating medium. For instance, when a string is plucked at a certain pitch level, it will vibrate as a whole, and at the same time will vibrate in segments: while the entire length of the string is racing back and forth, there are smaller subsidiary occurrences taking place in half the string length, in a quarter of the length, and so forth. On the oscilloscope the picture will no longer be a series of smooth curves, but each of the large curves will have superimposed upon it the effects of the segment vibrations, thus changing the outline of the main vibration, but changing each of these main vibrations in the same way so that each mountain and each valley will appear identical. This presence of overtones superimposed on the fundamental vibration is what gives character to the tone; it is what we hear as the *tone quality* and what permits us to associate a given tone with the instrument or voice that is producing it.

The foregoing is an attempt to boil down basic information that would take up many pages in a textbook on acoustics. For the scientifically-minded student, independent study in such textbooks is recommended. For the less inquisitive student, who feels he might become more befuddled by delving deeper into the technical physical basis of sound, here is a summary: (1) the *frequency* (speed) of the vibration gives us the *pitch* level; (2) the *amplitude* (size) gives us the *volume* of the musical sound; (3) the *complexity* (shape) of the sound waves gives us the distinctive *tone quality* of the medium of expression.

PART II

# The Five Fundamentals of Music

# The Five Fundamentals

TO BE completely effective most of the music we hear depends on five fundamentals: melody, harmony, rhythm, timbre, and form. The statement "most of the music" in the above sentence is used advisedly, for there are certain exceptions as there are to almost every rule or blanket statement. Several examples should substantiate this qualifying statement. For instance, a bugle playing *Taps* can be a fine experience musically as well as emotionally, but here harmony is omitted. The Gregorian chant of the Early Christian Church is excellent from a musical as well as from a religious point of view although it lacks both harmony and rhythm. And the street beat of a good drum section in a marching band can thrill the listener, with neither melody nor harmony present. But these are the exceptions, and the music we normally hear on radio or television or in recordings or concerts will have all five of the fundamentals mentioned.

These fundamentals do not stand alone, but are completely interdependent; it is the hearing of all five either consciously or unconsciously that makes our listening experience more pleasant.

Certain of the fundamentals may appeal to some individuals to a greater degree than do others, but the fact remains that all of them are necessary to give us a complete musical picture. The statement has often been made in criticism of the type of teaching suggested by this book that if one studies any of the fundamentals and attempts to listen to and for it alone in musical experiences he will miss the greater enjoyment of the complete composition. In contradiction to this point of view it has worked out in thousands of instances that if a student gives his attention judiciously and actively to each of the fundamentals until he can follow that part of the music with little difficulty, he will ultimately be able to hear the entire composition with each of the five fundamentals adding to his enjoyment in a way proportionate to its importance in the composition itself. And this is likely to happen much sooner and with more satisfying results than if he simply sits back and lets the music as a whole take its course.

CHAPTER 4

# *Timbre*

TIMBRE is that quality of music which permits us to distinguish one instrument from another, or from the human voice. As previously stated this quality depends upon the shape or complexity of the sound waves, which, in turn, derive their complexity from the materials used to produce the tone. The violin gives one sort of tone, the piano another, because of the construction of these two instruments and the method used in producing the tones thereon. The timbre of the violin and that of the piano are far different even to the least-trained ear, and it is impossible to conceive of anyone without serious hearing defects mistaking the two, if he knows in advance that one comparative sound is to come from the violin and the other from the piano.

The word *timbre* comes into our musical vocabulary from the French, and is adopted for use here because of its brevity, for it takes the place of an English equivalent that can only be given in a lengthier phrase: "tone quality plus tone color." The next logical step is to differentiate between tone quality and tone color, which together produce the *timbre,* for the purpose of proving to ourselves that it is really the combination of the two that "permits us to distinguish one instrument from another, or from the human voice."

The tone quality, which has its basis in the complexity of the sound waves, can serve alone as the factor that permits us to make a decision about what type of voice or instrument we are hearing. But if we add our interpretation of tone color to the tone quality, such recognition becomes easier. While tone quality is the actual sound heard, which is dependent upon the materials of the instrument or the music-making mechanism of the voice as heard by us and translated psychologically, tone color refers to our interpretation of these same sounds in the light of our experience, which has come down to us through the years and creeps up on us unconsciously. We describe the trumpet tone as "brassy and piercing." This refers to the tone quality and is aptly descriptive because of the metal composition of the instrument, its size and therefore comparatively high range among the instruments of the brass family, and the fact that the normal tone of the trumpet is produced by rapid lip vibrations backed up by no inconsiderable amount of wind, which sets the instrument in musical motion. But we can also say "the trumpet has a martial tone." This is also descriptively true when we consider the normal use of the instrument, but in this case the modifying adjective does not refer to the actual sound produced but to our interpretation of that sound: when we have heard bands in parade, or have heard the background music in the movies when a military scene is on the screen we have heard the trumpet as either the predominating instrument or, at least, one of the several predominating instruments. Composers have realized this natural use of the trumpet and this interpretation of its sound, and have scored for the trumpet when they represented things martial as long as they have been composing and perhaps before, for the practice may stem back to the famous days of Jericho when the trumpet played no mean part in the battle. Obviously, if a martial spirit is to be created in the minds of listeners, the composer will use trumpets and drums rather than give us a recital of muted violins and flutes. So, without being taught, we tend to hitch up a tone quality with one or several uses that have become traditional for a given instrument; this coloring suggested by the tone and the actual sound of the tone itself become intermingled in our minds. Thus "tone quality and tone color" together equal *timbre*.

In the discussion above, the phrase "one or several uses" occurred. The trumpet, and its martial sound served as an example of a single usage. The sound of the oboe can help explain the "several uses." The oboe has a reedy, nasal, penetrating sound, all of which descriptive words refer to the actual tone quality of the instrument, which is caused by the slightly conical bore and by the rapid vibrations of the double reed that sets the air in motion. But in addition the oboe has an oriental sound, which is a matter of tone color, due to the fact that composers have used the oboe when they wished to give an oriental feeling or coloring to the music.[1] But the oboe is also said to have a pastoral sound. Here we get a background of shepherds' pipes, and an attempt by the composer to come near to the sounds of these pipes of antiquity on our modern instrument when wishing to portray a quiet pastoral scene. In either case, oriental or pastoral, the usage of the instrument should and will act as an addition to the actual quality of the sound in helping us to analyze and distinguish the tones we hear produced by the oboe, to the extent that when it is used even without reference to either of the two color interpretations we may still have an easier time in distinguishing the timbre peculiar to it.

There are several statements of a cautionary nature that should be made. One is that every musical instrument differs from every

[1] This also has a historical background, because of the Asiatic forerunners of our present oboe: the musette used in connection with Egyptian dancing girl side shows at the circus is partial proof.

other one of the same type to some degree. This degree will probably be so slight that it will not be noticed (except, perhaps, by the oscilloscope), but for a larger degree compare the tone of a Stradivarius violin with that of the "fifteen-dollars-including-ten-lessons" type. Also, the instrument will sound different in the hands of different performers: Heifetz versus you on the above-mentioned Stradivarius would be an example. A third idea to keep in mind is that an instrument with the same capable performer may sound different if heard in actual recital in a small hall, a large auditorium, or outdoors, or over the air or on a recording. And in the last two instances the type of radio or record player will cause actual differences in the sound as it is heard. These differences may seem to add up to insurmountable odds in a listening program, but do not let that worry you, for the sound produced by a competent performer on a good instrument, whether on records or the radio, or in the actual presence of the listener, indoors or out, will sound so much more like the instrument in question than it will like any other that the distinguishing of that instrument from all others is quite possible for the average ear.

In reading in the field of acoustics you might come across the statement that there is no such thing as a distinctive tone quality for any one instrument, the implication being that each instrument has a series of qualities dependent upon the part of the instrument used from the point of view of range, plus other factors suggested in the preceding paragraph. While the acousticians are scientifically correct, it is still true that a trumpet will sound more like a trumpet than it will a French horn or a clarinet or a piano, and that for our purposes of listening to the produced sounds we may take a nonscientific approach and talk about the specific timbre of a trumpet or any other instrument with full justification.

Having made the above statement, which is not a contradiction, but only an attempt at simplification, it is only fair to the acoustician to elaborate. Every instrument can produce a series of chromatic tones from the lowest note possible on it because of its construction to the highest possible.[2] In the case of practically all of these instruments the extreme ends of the instrumental range are used far less than the notes in the middle registers. There are two reasons for this: first, it is technically difficult to produce the extremes (particularly the upper extreme), which will often lead to an inaccurate pitch; second, if a sound that lies in an extreme range of an instrument is wanted, there is often another instrument that can produce the same pitch in its middle register, with a timbre close enough to that desired so that it will satisfy the composer. For example, the low notes of a piccolo overlap in the musical scale range those in the middle register of a flute. The average composer, then, will use the piccolo in its middle and upper parts and will switch to the better-sounding flute when notes in the lower and overlapping range are desired.

In your listening program remember that the most representative tones on any instrument are the middle tones away from the extreme ends of the instrument, that these are the ones most used by the composer and therefore most often heard by you, to which you can safely assign your mental tag for the differentiation of the various voices and instruments. Recorded examples for listening purposes take into consideration this most representative use of each instrument in its normal playing range.

## *Objective Listening*

THE WHOLE PURPOSE of the text of this book is to help the reader to listen objectively and in a discriminating manner to musical compositions. Facts about music mean nothing in the appreciation

[2] This, of course, refers to melodic instruments, and does not include many members of the percussion family.

of music if simply presented and learned as abstract facts, but when applied to the music heard these same facts should do much to increase enjoyment. At the end of each section of discussion there is a list of recordings that will serve as examples of the subject under discussion. Through the use of these records the listener should be able to build up a repertory based on discrimination.

For our purposes it is both unnecessary and unwise to attempt to memorize the suggested selections, for by so doing you will be able to discern the important fundamentals of only those records you have listened to again and again. If a half-dozen records are suggested as examples for any specific feature, it would be far more advantageous to listen to each of these records once than to listen to one of them six times. For example, if you are trying to recognize the timbre of the English horn, you should listen to as many examples given for the English horn as possible, and not limit yourself to the *Largo* movement of the *From the New World Symphony*. Otherwise, you might be able to tell that the English horn was being used each time you heard that particular composition through association with the melody, but might fail in such recognition when the English horn was being used in any other compositions. Be careful not to let yourself give recognition by melodic association; rather think of the tone as you listen to it as something abstract—something that is an entity within itself that may appear in other selections of a different nature, but that will still be that particular and peculiar timbre of a certain voice or instrument, no matter what its setting.

Insofar as possible the appended lists of recorded material include only those numbers available through the usual sales channels at the time of this book's revision. Without doubt some good examples from the past have been omitted, but there is no use listing materials that are not to be had except as collectors' items. A list of records available even five years ago might include many items now unobtainable. For reasons best known to themselves many of the more than five hundred recording studios have dropped from production, and from their catalogues, certain titles that we might have expected to be permanent items. Also, some recording companies specializing in certain types of music have had spectacular success in their inaugural products, only to prove short-lived. And finally, the success of tape recordings may have something to do with the constant change in the month-by-month catalogue of recorded music.

Your listening program is based on the use of phonograph record (or tapes) for obvious reasons. With such recordings you can hear what you want when you want it, and listen to repetitions in whole or in part (although the latter is not recommended) as often as necessary to get the point involved. Music on radio and television is recommended as an adjunct to recordings. On many programs there are selections that tie in with various aspects of the art. The need is to know what you are listening to, and to have an idea of the specific characteristics you should objectively attend to.

The emphasis on the use of recordings or tape does not suggest the elimination of live performances. Far from it; an actual demonstration of performance on the cello, for instance, is much more valuable in learning the recognition of cello timbre than a lecture describing the instrument, its performance possibilities, its music, and its history, with the timbre shown by use of recordings, no matter how thorough the lecture might be or how fine the recordings used.

In any study a good rule of pedagogy is to go from the known

[3] This statement is true as applied to the first part of this course, which is the logical approach to music through its fundamentals. The second half of the course, in which the styles of the various periods and of particular composers are studied, will give an opportunity to use the radio to better advantage, for there it is important to listen to complete works as such, instead of the preliminary listening to fundamentals as they appear in these compositions.

to the unknown. Therefore the timbres of specific instruments will start with a study of the most common and the most ancient of instruments, and the one each of us plays with varying degrees of skill and satisfaction: the human voice.

## *VOCAL TIMBRE*

The human voice is an instrument subject to the same rules of acoustics as are instruments made of wood or metal. It is also the instrument that varies the most in the tone produced. Those human beings blessed with fine vocal instruments are our potentially great singers; those who not only have the instruments, but learn to use them correctly and take good care of them are our actual great singers. It is not necessary here to go into the physiology of the instrument: that can be found in any good book on singing. Nor is it necessary to go into the mechanics of producing tones with these vocal instruments: in this case there are almost as many methods suggested as there are vocal teachers. But it is important to remember that the human voice is actually an instrument in its own right, functioning to produce musical tones, and that these tones have been used by composers in songs, operas, oratorios, and other vocal media either alone or in combination with other voices or with other instruments. A knowledge of the various types of voices and the musical possibilities of these voices will aid us in an appreciation of the great amount of fine vocal literature available.

As music developed centuries ago, group singing was done in unison, or in octave-unison, the latter term meaning that if both unchanged voices and adult male voices were singing together they would sing the same tune, though an octave apart. However, with the development of harmony (in which all voices did not sing the same melody) voices came to be classified according to range. The timbre of the voice depends somewhat on this highness or lowness of the voice, just as the timbre of the various stringed instruments from the violin down to the string bass depends to some degree on the range of those instruments.

When part singing came into reality in the field of music there was a natural division of voices into four categories, which was a sufficient number of different vocal ranges to take care of the four-part harmony that is still the basis of a large percentage of our vocal music, as it was at that time. The four divisions of range from top to bottom are soprano, alto, tenor and bass. The soprano and alto represent the high and low of the female voice or the unchanged male voice; the tenor and bass are the high and low of the changed male voice, apparent after the physiological metamorphosis of the male human being in the adolescent period.

As time went on, it was discovered that many voices had in their range neither the necessary top notes of the soprano and the tenor, nor the rich low notes of the alto and bass. And yet these voices were of fine quality and usable in a number of ways. Additional range classifications were then necessary, which gives us the standard classification set forth below, from high to low with the two intermediate voices added to the four basic voices:

SOPRANO
mezzo-soprano
ALTO
-----
TENOR
baritone
BASS

These are now considered the six basic ranges of voice classifications, in spite of some of the terminology used in advertising by concert singers. The more common descriptive phrases are here given, so that you will not be mystified if you run across them:

*Contralto:* originally there was the implication that this was a particularly low alto voice; at the present time the two terms are practically synonymous.

*Lyric baritone:* a voice having some of the range characteristics of both the baritone and the tenor.

*Bass-baritone:* just what is implied: both bass and baritone qualities.

*Basso profundo:* this suggests that the singer is very proud of his extremely low notes and doesn't want that fact forgotten.

In the six major voice classifications listed above the presence of lower-case letters in the two most recent additions—mezzo-soprano and baritone—should not lead to a supposition that these voices are either inferior in quality or in numbers. As far as prevalence is concerned there are many more mezzo-sopranos and baritones than there are voices of the other four classifications. For confirmation ask the music director who holds tryouts for either men's or women's glee clubs: there is always a preponderance of the middle registers in both the male and female divisions.

In addition to these voice divisions according to range there is a further subdivision, particularly in the higher voices. The soprano and tenor have more flexibility due to their physiological make-up than do the lower voices: more than a century ago composers discovered that these voices were able to sing types of music that differed in kind though in the same range.

As a result the sopranos are subdivided into three categories, dependent upon various vocal factors that make their particular voices capable of performing certain types of vocal literature better than others. These classifications are called *coloratura, dramatic,* and *lyric* sopranos. It should be understood that a great soprano will sing chiefly that type of literature that best fits her vocal possibilities, but this does not necessarily mean that she is limited to that type of literature to the complete exclusion of the other types. But since she has the qualifications for specialization, and since there is ample good literature in each of these specializations, it is natural that she will normally sing in her public performances that type of music that will best show off the particular qualities of her voice.

The *coloratura* soprano is a voice that has as its peculiar quality the ability to execute rapid runs and trills: the key word is the flexibility of the vocal processes. Italian composers in particular favored this flexible type of soprano voice, with the result that the leading soprano roles in many Italian operas require a coloratura. Composers have also written songs designed to give the coloratura soprano a chance to display her prowess. It is the type of voice correctly although perhaps unkindly, described by the term "vocal gymnastics."

The *dramatic* soprano excels in expressing in her singing all of the emotions of human behavior. Most soprano roles in opera (except those calling for a coloratura) call for a dramatic soprano; a wealth of song material also utilizes the histrionic ability of the dramatic soprano voice.

The chief characteristic of the *lyric* soprano is sheer beauty of tone. This does not detract from the beauty of the other two types, for to be great they must have beauty of tone with their other attributes. But the lyric soprano depends on the beauty alone, without additional flexibility or great emotional expressiveness. Folk songs and much composed song literature are worthy vehicles for the lyric soprano.

In like manner the tenor voice has been subdivided by experience and tradition, and tenors will specialize in the type of literature best suited to their vocal equipment. It is difficult to find a unanimity of terminology according to various writers on the subject, but the three divisions can best be characterized as *lyric*, *dramatic* (or *heroic*), and *robusto*.

The *lyric* tenor, like the lyric soprano excels in the sheer beauty of the tone, and will therefore choose music that has slow-moving melodies with many sustained notes, so that this beauty will have a chance to be displayed. Many of our best-known radio tenors in the field of musical entertainment belong in this category; the Irish tenor would be of this type.

The *dramatic* tenor is very often a tenor by development, because of the difficulties involved in some of the operatic roles, particularly in the Wagnerian operas, that he is required to sing. He often is an individual who started his career as a high baritone and who through arduous practice has added enough high notes so that he can sing these taxing roles, which require a tremendous endurance that the lighter natural tenor voice often lacks.

The tenor *robusto,* obviously of Italian origin, is a big tenor voice with tremendous power in the high registers. If you have heard a voice that almost literally causes the chandelier to shake you have probably been listening to a tenor robusto going at full force.

Here we should pause in our discussion of musical terms to think about the meaning of words. In order to describe certain musical sounds it has been necessary to use good common English words (as, for example, the "big" tenor voice mentioned in the preceding paragraph). But there is always the possibility that any descriptive word used in the text might have a different connotation or at least a different shade of meaning in your mind. Therefore, when descriptive words are used in relation to sounds, we are treading on dangerous ground. On hearing a musical selection you should test to see if the description used fits in with your interpretation of the sound; do this objectively, and if you find that it fails to describe to you what you hear, substitute your own words or phrase. Your descriptions, because they *are* your descriptions, will better help you to understand and recall the phase of the music in question.

As you gain the ability to differentiate among voices, both by range and by type, and as you listen to the various styles of music that these voices are given to sing, you should get more pleasure from, and have more appreciation for, all of the phases of vocal literature, which is one of the two major divisions of our entire field of musical expression, with instrumental music as the other. Continued listening will also give you a basis for your own evaluation of the various voices in any particular classification. As a result, the more listening you do the more chance there is of your finding your own likes and dislikes, either in types or in individual performers, which will lead in future years to discriminating listening to those things that please you most. In your listening be fair to yourself: enter this listening experience with an open mind and make your decisions after you have had an opportunity to hear numerous examples in each field.

### *SUGGESTED LISTENING*

NOTE: Some of the greatest voices of this century belong to singers who predated the era of electrical recordings, but whose singing was recorded by the less desirable mechanical means. Since some of these fine examples of great vocal performance have been reissued on LP records from the original master platters they are included in these listings. (You should allow for the difference in recording in order to recognize the worth of the voice itself.) In addition, some of the more recent vocalists who have passed their prime, but who were the great voices of the immediate past, did record on the newer process, and were well represented on 78 r.p.m. records, but have not yet been brought over to the 33⅓ speed. Watch for new LP releases of such men as Lawrence Tibbett, baritone, and Alexander Kipnis, bass, and add them to the list, for both should be well represented here.

In the following listings, specific works are suggested, followed by the names of some of the singers worth hearing in these works.

Any vocalist listed will serve as an example of the type of voice in question.

*Coloratura soprano*

Bishop: *Lo, Here the Gentle Lark* (Lily Pons)
Delibes: *Bell Song,* from *Lakmé* (Anna Moffo, Maria Callas)
Donizetti: The Mad Scene, from *Lucia di Lammermoor* (Patrice Munsel, Erna Sack, Joan Sutherland, Callas)
Donizetti: *Regnava nel silenzio,* from *Lucia di Lammermoor* (Munsel)
Meyerbeer: *Ombra leggiera,* from *Dinorah* (Callas)
Mozart: Queen of the Night Aria, from *The Magic Flute* (Pons)
Rossini: *Una voce poco fa,* from *Barber of Seville* (Pons, Sack, Munsel, Callas)
Verdi: *Sempre libera,* from *La Traviata* (Amelita Galli-Curci)

*Dramatic soprano*

Giordano: *La mamma morta,* from *Andrea Chénier* (Maria Callas)
Mascagni: *Voi lo sapete,* from *Cavalleria Rusticana* (Helen Traubel, Zinka Milanov)
Ponchielli: *Suicidio!,* from *La Gioconda* (Traubel, Milanov)
Puccini: *Un bel di, vedremo,* from *Madame Butterfly* (Dorothy Kirsten, Lucrezia Bori, Licia Albanese, Callas)
Puccini: *Vissi d'arte,* from *Tosca* (Kirsten, Traubel, Maria Jeritza)
Verdi: *Ritorna vincitor,* from *Aïda* (Traubel, Callas)
Verdi: *O patria mia,* from *Aïda* (Milanov, Renata Tebaldi)
Verdi: *Pace, pace,* from *La Forza del Destino* (Leontyne Price, Milanov, Callas)
Wagner: *Brunnhilde's Immolation,* from *Götterdämmerung* (Kirsten Flagstad, Eileen Farrel, Traubel)
Wagner: Love Duet, from *Tristan und Isolde* (Flagstad, Traubel, with dramatic tenor)
Wagner: Bridal Scene, from *Lohengrin* (Flagstad, with dramatic tenor)
Wagner: Kundry-Parsifal Duet, from *Parsifal* (Flagstad, with dramatic tenor)
Weber: *Ocean, Thou Mighty Monster,* from *Oberon* (Birgit Nilsson)

*Lyric soprano*

Charpentier: *Depuis le jour,* from *Louise* (Licia Albanese)
Handel: *Oh Sleep, Why Dost Thou Leave Me,* from *Semele* (Dorothy Mayor)
Handel: *He Shall Feed His Flock,* from the *Messiah* (Isobel Baillie, Elsie Morison)
Mozart: Songs (Erna Berger)
Mozart: *Ruhe sanft,* from *Zaide* (Barbara Troxell)
Puccini: *Addio di Mimi,* from *La Bohème* (Albanese)
Schubert: *Heidenröslein* (Elizabeth Schumann, Berger)
Schubert: Songs (Elizabeth Schwarzkopf)
Spanish Folk Songs (Victoria de los Angeles)
Villa-Lobos: *Bachianas Brasileiras No. 5* (Bidu Sayao, de los Angeles)

*Mezzo-soprano*

Bach: *Erbarme dich, mein Gott,* from *St. Matthew Passion* (Jennie Tourel)
Debussy: *Trois Chansons de Bilitis* (Tourel)
Gershwin: *Bess, You Is My Woman Now,* from *Porgy and Bess* (Risë Stevens, with baritone)
Gershwin: *Summertime,* from *Porgy and Bess* (Stevens)
Mahler: *Songs of a Wayfarer* (Blanche Thebom)
Ravel: *Chansons Madicasses* (Tourel)
Saint-Saëns: *My Heart at Thy Sweet Voice,* from *Samson et Dalila* (Gladys Swarthout, Stevens, Thebom)
Songs of Auvergne (Swarthout)
Spanish and Portuguese Songs (Tourel)

*Alto*

Bach: *Kreuze und Krone,* from *Contata # 12* (Marian Anderson)
Brahms: *Four Serious Songs* (Kathleen Ferrier)
Brahms: *Alto Rhapsody* (Ferrier, and men's voices)
English Songs (Ferrier)
Falla: *El Amor Brujo* (Carol Brice)
Handel: *O Thou that Tellest Good Tidings to Zion,* from the *Messiah* (Ferrier)
Handel: *Return, O God of Hosts,* from *Samson* (Ferrier)

Mendelssohn: *But the Lord Is Mindful of His Own,* from *St. Paul* (Ernestine Schumann-Heink, Anderson)
Schubert: *Erlkönig* (Elena Nikolaida)
Schubert: *Death and the Maiden* (Anderson)
Six Sacred Songs (Nikolaida)
Six Schubert Songs (Nikolaida)
Spirituals (Anderson)

*Lyric tenor*

Bach-Gounod: *Ave Maria* (James Melton)
Bizet: *Agnus Dei* (Melton)
Franck: *Panis Angelicus* (John McCormack, Melton)
Handel: *Ombra mai fu,* from *Xerxes* (Kenneth McKellar)
Handel: *Behold and See,* from the *Messiah* (James Johnston, Richard Lewis)
Schubert: *Ave Maria* (McCormack)
Schubert: *Du Bist die Ruh'* (Roland Hayes)
Spirituals (Hayes)

*Dramatic tenor*

Wagner: *In Fernem Land,* from *Lohengrin* (Set Svanholm, Richard Crooks, Lauritz Melchior)
Wagner: *Preislied,* from *Die Meistersinger* (Svanholm)
Wagner: Siegmund's Monologue, from *Die Walküre* (Svanholm)
Wagner: Rome Narrative, from *Tannhäuser* (Hans Hopf, Svanholm)
Wagner: Bridal Scene, from *Lohengrin* (Kurt Baum, with dramatic soprano, Lauritz Melchior, with dramatic soprano)
Wagner: Kundry-Parsifal Duet, from *Parsifal* (Melchior, with dramatic soprano)
Wagner: Love Duet, from *Tristan und Isolde* (Melchior, with dramatic soprano)

*Tenor robusto*

Leoncavallo: *Vesti la Giubba,* from *I Pagliacci* (Enrico Caruso, Jan Peerce, Jussi Bjoerling)
Mascagni: *Addio alla madre,* from *Cavalleria Rusticana* (Bjoerling, Caruso)

Meyerbeer: *O Paradiso,* from *L'Africaine* (Ferruccio Tagliavini, Caruso)
Ponchielli: *Cielo e mar,* from *La Gioconda* (Peerce, Bjoerling, Caruso)
Puccini: *Che gelida manina,* from *La Bohème* (Giuseppe di Stefano)
Puccini: *E lucevan le stelle,* from *Tosca* (Tagliavini, Beniamino Gigli, Bjoerling, di Stefano)
Verdi: *Celeste Aïda,* from *Aïda* (Caruso, Gigli)
Verdi: *La donna e mobile,* from *Rigoletto* (Mario del Monaco, Bjoerling, Peerce)
Verdi: Temple Scene, from *Aïda* (Giovanni Martinelli, with bass)
Verdi: *Solenne in questa ora,* from *La Forza del Destina* (Bjoerling, with baritone)

*Baritone*

Gershwin: *Where Is My Bess?,* from *Porgy and Bess* (Robert Merrill, William Warfield)
Gershwin: *Bess, You Is My Woman Now,* from *Porgy and Bess* (Merrill, with mezzo-soprano)
Handel: *Where E'er You Walk,* from *Semele* (Lawrence Tibbett)
Leoncavallo: *Prologue* to *I Pagliacci* (Leonard Warren, Frank Guarrera, Merrill)
Massenet: *Salome! Salome!,* from *Herodiade* (John Charles Thomas)
Rossini: *Largo al factotum,* from *Barber of Seville* (Guarrera, Warren)
Schubert: Songs (Dietrich Fischer-Dieskau)
Schumann: Songs (Fischer-Dieskau)
Verdi: *Eri tu,* from *Un Ballo in Maschera* (Merrill, Warren)
Verdi: *Io l'ho perduta,* from *Don Carlos* (Merrill, with tenor robusto)
Verdi: *Solenne in questa ora,* from *La Forza del Destino* (Antonio Scotti, with tenor robusto)
Wagner: *Die Frist ist Um,* from the *Flying Dutchman* (Hans Hotter)
Wagner: *Wotan's Farewell,* from *Die Walküre* (Hotter)
Wagner: *Wahn! Wahn! Uberall Wahn!,* from *Die Meistersinger* (Friedrich Schorr, Hotter)

*Bass*

Brahms: *Ein Wanderer* (Alexander Kipnis)
Brahms: *Dein Blaues Auge* (Kipnis)
Brahms: *Meine Liebe ist Grün* (Kipnis)
Halévy: *Si la rigueur et la vengeance,* from *La Juive* (Ezio Pinza)
Handel: *The People That Walked in Darkness,* from the *Messiah* (Norman Walker)
Mussorgsky: *Song of the Flea* (Boris Christoff)
Mussorgsky: Death or Boris, from *Boris Godunov* (Maxim Mikhailov, Feodor Chaliapin, Pinza)
Rossini: *La Calunnia,* from *Barber of Seville* (Cesare Siepi, Chaliapin, Pinza)
*Song of the Volga Boatmen* (Christoff, Chaliapin)
Tchaikovsky: *Prince Gremin's Air,* from *Eugen Onegin* (Christoff)
Verdi: Temple Scene, from *Aïda* (Pinza, with tenor robusto)

## *INSTRUMENTAL TIMBRE*

Instruments are voices, and voices are instruments, and later on you will find the two words "voice" and "instrument" used interchangeably. But for the present consider the human voice not only as a particular instrument but as one separate from the rest. In this section the word "instrument" will have its general meaning: "a mechanical contrivance for the production of musical sounds."

All instruments may be divided into certain general classifications, primarily according to the method of initiating the sound waves that are the musical tones we hear. These four major classifications are string, woodwind, brass, and percussion. A few common instruments may be a combination of two of these, but, by and large, instruments, particularly of the orchestra and band, will fall into one of the classifications mentioned above.

Our first approach to instrumental study will be an analysis of those instruments commonly used in the symphony orchestra. This initial approach is logical because most of the great literature for instrumental groups has been written for the orchestra or for smaller combinations of instruments that are found within it. This orchestral approach is done with full realization of the ever-growing popularity of the band, particularly in our schools, for since we are suggesting the use of recorded material, and since our great output of instrumental music has been for the orchestra, we find that there is an overwhelming predominance of orchestra recordings in comparison to records of band music. In addition, the orchestra contains not only the woodwinds, brasses, and percussion instruments of the band (with some exceptions), but the very important string group as well.

The four divisions of similar instruments in the orchestra are known as the four choirs. (This is the first of many musical terms that have several meanings and applications. This is unfortunate but true. Be sure to understand each meaning as it comes into your musical vocabulary.) The church choir is a group of similar instruments: human voices. In like manner each orchestra choir is a group of similar instruments—similar in this case because of the method of producing the musical sounds.

## *The String Choir*

THE MOST IMPORTANT CHOIR in the orchestra is the string choir. This statement is based on three considerations: (1) the historical background of the orchestra; (2) the relative number of these instruments used in the orchestra; and (3) the dependence of orchestral music on the string timbre.

Vocal music reached a high state of development at a much earlier date than instrumental music, simply because the human voice was always a reality, whereas instruments had to be constructed and then perfected before they were satisfactory from an esthetic standpoint. Historically, the orchestra came into being as an adjunct to the opera. From its start as a purely accompanying group, wherein the instruments duplicated the vocal parts, the orchestra was gradually permitted to play its own music divorced from the vocal score, in the form of overtures and entr'acte music. As the instrumental group received recognition as a musical unit in its own right, and as it became further liberated from the opera score, composers began to turn their talents toward writing specifically for the instrumental group.[4]

In the early days of instrumental combinations the strings predominated. The stringed instruments had reached a state of perfection long before the instruments of the other choirs did, partly because they were the products of skilled craftsmen who worked with wood, and did not involve the mechanics necessary for true-toned performance on the woodwinds and brasses. Since the strings were in as high a state of perfection at that time as they are today the composers naturally emphasized their use. Woodwinds and brasses were sometimes used, but were not as satisfactory as the strings for two reasons: (1) the mechanics of the valves, holes, and keys were comparatively crude so that correct

[4] Composers, being anxious to have their music performed, will naturally write for an established medium, for if they compose for too unusual a combination there is the likelihood that the music will never be heard. You may have heard of the embryo composer who decided to write a *concerto grosso* for sixteen Hammond organs: it is unlikely that this would ever get a hearing except in the Hammond factory, and if there happened to be sixteen of these instruments in the same concert hall it is just as unlikely that anyone would want to hear them.

intonation was often as dependent upon luck as on skill; and (2) some of the instruments had not reached that stage in their construction whereby they could play all of the chromatic notes of the scale, hence were not very useful because of musical limitations.

As the orchestra developed it became evident that the timbre of the strings was basic for the character of the ensemble. It also became evident that the proportion of stringed instruments must be kept large in relation to the other choirs so that this string tone could predominate even when members of the other three choirs were introduced and used in the ensemble.

The string choir includes those instruments whose tone is produced by the vibration of a string. In every case the strings are stretched over a chamber of air within the body of the instrument which acts as a sounding box and causes the sound to be increased in intensity by the sympathetic vibration of this air within the sounding box. Stringed instruments may be further subdivided on the basis of the normal method of starting the string to vibrate: the two groups are the bowed instruments and the plucked instruments. The two groups have the uneven ratio of about 60 to 1 in the symphony orchestra, with the harp being the only plucked instrument included in the symphony family, but the division is much more nearly even when you take into consideration the nonsymphonic guitar, the banjo, the ukulele and others of the "less-heroic instruments" of a similar nature.

To have some idea of the relative number of instruments of each type that are used in the symphony orchestra to achieve the fine balance of tone of that organization is important. This balance of instrumentation has become rather well standardized after a gradual and experimental approach throughout the history of the orchestra. The list used here was derived by taking an average of various major symphony orchestras in this country, when they were manned so that they could perform most of the music that has been written for the orchestra. If you should see an orchestra in performance or on television that does not conform exactly with the count listed, it might be for one of four reasons: (1) certain conductors prefer a slightly different string balance; (2) the music being played in a given concert might have been written during the developing period of orchestral history, and thus might not call for the full present-day quota; (3) the music being played might require several more performers than the standard; and (4) economic difficulties might have caused the orchestra management to cut down on the size of the personnel of some sections, to the probable dismay of the conductor.

The string choir of this average large symphony orchestra would consist of the following:

| | | |
|---|---|---|
| Bowed instruments | | 60 |
| violins (1st violins) | 16 | |
| " (2nd violins) | 14 | |
| violas | 12 | |
| 'cellos | 10 | |
| basses | 8 | |
| Plucked instrument | | 1 |
| harp | 1 | |
| Total: | | 61 |

Since this standard orchestra will include a total of about ninety performers, the relative importance of the string choir can be seen by the fact that there are twice as many string players as there are performers in the other three choirs combined.

### THE VIOLIN

If for no other reason than by sheer force of numbers the *violin* is the main instrument of the orchestra. But there are other reasons as well: the expressiveness of the instrument, the beauty of its timbre both in its quality and in its various colorings, and the technical possibilities in various types of performance.

In the numerical listing above you will notice the subdivision of the violins into "1st" and "2nd." The personnel of these sections will also be so listed on an orchestra program. This is the only section of the orchestra in which this distinction is made. It is done purposely, for distinct parts are written for each group, sometimes playing together but generally complementing each other. If we assign vocal terminology to the string choir, we would say correctly that the violins, through this division, are both the soprano and the alto voices of the ensemble. Certain misapprehensions concerning first violins versus second violins should be cleared up: (1) there is no difference between the two in the size, the tuning, or the technique of the instrument; (2) the players in the second violin section must be as proficient as those in the first violin section and there is no stigma attached to being a second violinist.[5]

The violin is constructed from more than seventy separate pieces of wood; this is not obvious since many of them are inside the instrument for strengthening purposes. The top of the instrument is made of a loose-grained wood, such as pine, which is also used in the interior parts including the sound post; the sides, back, neck and bridge are fashioned from finer-grained and harder wood, such as maple or sycamore; the finger board, tailpiece, nut and pegs are of ebony, which is still harder. Each of these woods is selected for a specific reason. The loose-grained top permits an

[5] This erroneous idea probably cropped up from those who played in public-school orchestras and who played music that was so arranged that all instrumental students including the beginners might have a chance to participate in ensemble experience. In such cases the music for the second violin was written expressly for those who had not yet developed a good technique on the instrument and often consisted, for example, of the "pahs" in the "oom-pah-pah" of waltz rhythm. But in great symphonic works the music for the second violins can be and often is every bit as difficult and as interesting as the first violin music.

easier transmission of the sound waves from the strings and bridge through the top in order to set the air chamber and the outer air in motion. A sturdier wood but still a grained wood that will permit some vibration is required for strength in construction of the rest of the instrument. The harder wood is used where the strings through tension at each extremity or through pressure by the fingers would cause grooving of a softer material.

The four strings are made of one of several materials: sheep-gut, gut covered with copper, aluminum, or silver wire, wire itself, and more recently nylon. No matter what the material, the strings are of a thickness and are stretched to a tension that brings the best acoustical response from the instrument. The strings are tuned five notes apart (G-D-A-E from the low upwards), which gives a wide range of pitch levels.

In normal performance the violin string is set in motion and continued in motion by drawing the hairs of the bow across the string. This gives a continuous sound except for almost imperceptible pauses in tone when the direction of the bowing is changed. There are, however, many variations on this type of bowing and other ways that are used to produce a tone, and, while it is unnecessary to go into details concerning all of the various techniques employed by the violinist, it is well to understand the more common ones since they are used not only by the concert artist, but quite often by all members of the violin section of an orchestra. You will be able to hear many of these effects in the records listed.

*Col legno:* strike the strings with the wooden shaft of the bow, which will cause almost a clicking sound of the note.

*Double stops:* play two adjacent strings simultaneously, which gives the effect of a violin duet played on a single instrument.

*Harmonics:* the utilization of the vibrations of the string in its smaller segments. The technique calls for merely touching a string at a given point, with a finger of the left hand, rather than pressing it to the finger board; the resultant tone will be the pitch of one of the overtones, which may be eight or twelve or fifteen or more notes higher than the fundamental tone.

*Mute:* a device which is placed on the bridge of the violin, cutting down the strength of the vibration and cutting down on the ratio of some of the overtones, thus giving a softer tone with a slightly different timbre from the normal. The term *con sordino* means "with the mute," and *senza sordino* signifies "without the mute."

*Pizzicato:* to pluck the string with the finger, causing a sound similar to that made on one of the plucked instruments. (*Arco* means to return to normal bowing after the *pizzicato* has been used.)

*Spiccato:* produce a tone by bouncing the hair of the bow on the strings, giving short, sharp sounds.

Attention has been called to the bow many times in this discussion. It is a very important part of the violinist's equipment: a concert artist will pay many hundreds of dollars for a bow that suits his style of playing. It is actually a shaft of Brazilian Pernambuco wood (or other similar wood) which has been bent slightly from end to end by heat treatment. Horse hairs are attached to one end and to a screw mechanism at the other end, which permits the performer to tighten them slightly before playing. This tightening causes a desired elasticity in the shaft of the bow that is necessary for the performance of the various styles of bowing explained in the preceding paragraph.

If a fine bow costs many hundred dollars we should not be surprised that the price of a fine violin will go into multiples of ten thousand dollars. Violins made by the Amati family, by Stradivarius and the Guarnieri family in seventeenth- and eighteenth-century Italy, and by their counterparts in early Germany and France and England demand a very high price. This is no doubt due not only to the exquisite workmanship, and the mellowing of the instrumental tone through centuries of playing, but also to the fact that they are definite collectors' items. Excellent violins are made today at a much more reasonable figure.

### THE VIOLA

If the violin is considered to be both soprano and alto in its range, the *viola* would take its place as a tenor instrument, although these comparisons are only relative. The construction of the two instruments is similar, with the viola having an over-all extra length of about two and one-half inches and being proportionally larger throughout. The four strings are tuned five notes apart (C-G-D-A from the low upwards) with the lowest-pitched string five notes deeper than the lowest string of the violin. This makes the next three strings have the same pitches as the three lower strings of the violin, which suggests considerable duplication in pitch between the two instruments: the viola can play five low notes not found on the violin, and the violin has the same extended upper range not found on the viola. Why, then, should this instrument be used? For an answer we get the approximate relationship here that we have, for example, between the alto and the tenor voice. And, as in the tenor voice, we find the ability of the viola to play those low extra notes very important in music writing. We find also that there is a definite character to the viola timbre that cannot be duplicated on the violin.

This timbre of the viola is comparable in the beauty of its quality to that of the violin, but it lacks a certain amount of brilliance. The explanation of this becomes very involved with scientific acoustical reasons. A simplified explanation can be made as follows: when discussing the violin timbre mention was made of a definite relationship between the length of the strings, their thickness and their tension. But if this perfect ratio were used on the viola, the instrument would be tuned only three notes lower than the violin because of its only slightly larger size; conversely, if the perfect ratio were kept, and the instrument were tuned to the pitches now assigned to its strings, it would have to be several inches longer than its present dimensions. But since the viola is played in the same manner as the violin, with the instrument extended from between the chin and the collarbone, it would be too unwieldy to play if it were larger in size. And if the normal-sized viola had a range only three notes deeper than that of the violin, it would add but little to the string ensemble. So for matters of expediency in handling and the additional pitch range desirable we have an instrument that forgoes the perfect ratio with a resultant sound that lacks a certain amount of brilliance but does retain a very gracious string timbre.

Since the normal use of the viola in the orchestra is to carry an inner harmony part, the instrument will not be as obvious as is the violin when you listen to complete orchestrations. However, in recent years a number of good performers on the viola have given concert performances and made recordings which bring out the possibilities of the viola as a melodic solo instrument. This is fortunate, for it gives a better chance to compare the timbre of the viola with that of the other members of the string choir.

Because of the part it normally plays in symphonic works the viola has been called "the philosopher of the orchestra." This can be interpreted to mean that in spite of its harmonic importance it does its part in a quiet and calm way, and doesn't force itself upon your attention; it is one of those instruments that you don't notice particularly when the full orchestra is playing, but the lack of which would be most noticeable. You might think of the viola as the blocking back of the orchestra: its job isn't to carry the ball (the melody), but to add to the total effect and make it easier for someone else like the fleeter wingback (the violin) or fullback (the 'cello) to get in the limelight.

The various techniques listed for the violin also apply to the viola as they do to the 'cello and bass. It is played in the same position, and the bow is similar.

### THE 'CELLO

The apostrophe in the title given above has, until recently, been an important part of the word, for we Americans tend to be a bit careless in our terminology, and thus speak of the *'cello,* which is actually an abbreviation of the complete word *violoncello,* which is used by the Italians who invented the instrument, and, with slight terminal changes, by the French and Germans also. But more and more the apostrophe is being used less and less, and a person who now writes about the *cello* can be considered perfectly correct, although perhaps not quite as erudite as the *'cello* writers.

This instrument is a larger member of the string family—so large in fact, that it must be played with the performer seated, and the instrument held between his knees and resting on the floor. An adjustable spike on the lower end takes care of the disparity in the sizes of performers. The larger size of the 'cello demands a difference in manipulation, but the basic facts about the violin and viola apply equally to it. The size is also responsible for the lower pitch of this instrument compared to its smaller relations.

Like the violin and viola the 'cello strings are tuned to pitches five notes apart. While the string names are the same as those of the viola (C-G-D-A) each string is an octave (eight notes) below the similarly named string of the viola. This means that only the two upper strings of the 'cello encroach on the pitches played on the two lower strings of the viola.

The timbre of the 'cello is said to be the nearest approach of any instrument to the quality of the human voice. To give this statement the interpretation implied it might be wise to say that the 'cello timbre most nearly approaches the sound of a lovely human voice, for the instrument again has that ratio that made perfection of the violin, but which was skipped over by the viola. This means that not only is it a good basic instrument, but it is capable of melody-carrying and is given that assignment by many composers. After the first violin it is the most-used instrument in the string choir in passages that force themselves on the consciousness of the listener. As the violins and violas have been assigned vocal counterparts of the higher ranges, so the 'cello would be considered the baritone voice in its choir, but actually a lyric baritone that can soar to great heights in its solo passages.

### THE BASS

Again we have become careless, for this instrument has been variously called the contrabass, the double bass, and the string bass. But the word *bass* suffices and in order not to cause any confusion the bass of the brass choir will be called *tuba* when we get that far in our discussion.

This instrument is one of the best known of the string choir as far as its appearance is concerned, since it is also included in the dance orchestra. But dance-orchestra performance on the bass is not the characteristic use of the instrument in the symphony orchestra. In dance work the bass is played *pizzicato,* and while this effect is sometimes called for in symphonic music the instrument is usually played with the bow. In fact, most of the performance possibilities of the other stringed instruments are employed in string bass playing.

The peculiar characteristics of the bass derive from its size: it is so large that the performer must stand in order to reach and have control of the finger board. Because of the distance between finger positions, which comes from its size, the strings are tuned only four notes apart (E-A-D-G). Note that they are just the reverse of the names of the violin strings. The two lower strings are below the lowest playable note on the 'cello; the vocal range of the instrument is definitely a low bass, which is not surprising when we realize that the lowest tone on this instrument is within five notes of the lowest key on the standard full-sized piano.

The bass is usually assigned the job of taking care of the basic note of the chord construction: it acts as a sort of underpinning for the rest of the string choir, and often for the rest of the orchestra. Sometimes, though rarely, the basses are given a solo passage; when this is done it is generally to produce an effect that would be lost if any other instruments were used. It has a basically rugged timbre. One of its chief duties is to balance by its low notes the high notes of the violins and other soprano instruments. While not important as a melodic instrument, it is, like the viola, a very necessary instrument in the whole orchestral scheme of things and its absence would be very noticeable.

### THE HARP

Because it is the one plucked instrument in the orchestra and because of the type of music written for it recognition of the *harp* will probably be less confusing in a listening program than will that of almost any other orchestral instrument. It is not very often scored for by composers, but when it is used it is called on to furnish specific effects that can't be duplicated by any of the other instruments.

The forerunners of the harp go back to antiquity and its triangular form or slight variations of that form with the series of stretched strings of different tonalities were found in biblical times and probably existed before their presence was recorded by words or pictures. Egypt, Assyria, Greece, Ireland, Scotland, and Wales were among the countries that used these instruments to accompany their singers very early in their civilizations.

The mechanics of the modern harp are interesting. The side of the triangle next to the player is hollow wood, probably pine or spruce, which acts as the sounding board. Across the top of the triangle the strings (46 or 47 of them) are attached to double-action levers. These in turn are connected to rods that go down through the hollow pillar of sycamore wood on the far side of the triangle, and are in turn connected to pedals at the base of the instrument. The tuning of the strings can be likened to the white keys on the piano, with all but the single lowest key and the three highest ones on the piano included. They have the names of the notes of the musical scale: C-D-E-F-G-A-B-C-D etc. up to the highest F. Now for the mechanism: every A string is connected through the mechanism mentioned to the A pedal; every B string to the B pedal, and so on. Each pedal, in turn, has three positions in which it may be anchored. When the A pedal is in its upper position all of the A strings will sound as A flats: when the pedal is in its middle position the mechanism has changed all of the A strings so that they will now sound as A naturals; in its third position the pedal will cause all of these strings to sound as A sharps. Therefore each string has three different pitches regulated by the position of the corresponding pedal; this takes care of the tones represented by the black keys on the piano. Key signatures may worry pianists and performers on almost any instrument, but not the harpist. In order to play in the key of six sharps, for instance, she (it's generally a "she") sets all the pedals except the B pedal in the sharp position and the B pedal in the natural position before starting to play, and immediately forgets all about the key signature since the harp is now tuned to play in the key of six sharps!

Typical harp music calls for the *glissando* (in which the finger or thumb is drawn rapidly back and forth over the strings), broken chords, *arpeggios*, and other accompanying devices. The harp is often used as a solo instrument; when used in connection with a symphony orchestra or smaller ensemble it adds a most gratifying sparkle of tone color.

### STRINGS IN COMBINATION

Because of their timbre the stringed instruments are often used by themselves or in combinations as well as in the complete orchestra. There are several groupings that have been favorites over the years, the most favored by composers, performers, and listeners being the *string quartet.* This combination consists of two violins, a viola, and a 'cello. Literature for it has been composed by many of the great geniuses in the field of music writing, with the result that the fine music of the string quartet remains one of the most popular sources of enjoyment for the discriminating listener. It might seem that since there are four different sizes of bowed stringed instruments one of each would be used in the string quartet. But if both the 'cello and the bass were used, there would be too much music of the low pitches for the balance with the middle-range viola and the higher violin. Justification for the instrumentation of the quartet as constituted can be made in two ways: (1) a recall of the numbers of each instrument used to balance the string section of the symphony orchestra, and (2) the assignment of vocal ranges to the various instruments.

Another though somewhat less popular small combination utilizing some of the strings is known as the *piano trio,* consisting of violin, 'cello, and piano. This ensemble should not be judged by groups playing behind palms in swanky hotels or in the lobbies of summer resorts, but rather by the recordings of music by great composers performed by fine musicians.

The *string orchestra* as such, utilizing the string section of the symphony without help from the other choirs has also received considerable attention from the great composers, particularly those of the early days of orchestral composition. There are many fine recorded examples of the *concerto grosso* and other works in which the string orchestra is the playing medium.

## SUGGESTED LISTENING

### *Violin as a solo instrument*

Any violin concerto or independent solo by such performers as Zino Francescatti, Jascha Heifetz, Fritz Kreisler, Yehudi Menuhin, Nathan Milstein, David Oistrakh, Ruggiero Ricci, Tossy Spivakovsky, Isaac Stern, Joseph Szigeti.

### *Solo violin: examples of various techniques*

Kreisler: *Caprice Viennois* (double stops, spiccato bowing)
Grofé: *On the Trail*, from *Grand Canyon Suite* (after two opening measures, violin cadenza, using double stops, glissando, and almost complete range of the instrument)
Dvořák: *Humoresque*: double stops
Paganini: *Caprices*
- # 13: double stops
- # 14: double, triple, and quadruple stops, spiccato bowing
- # 15: double stops, in octaves
- # 18: double stops
- # 21: double stops
- # 22: double stops
- # 24, Variation I: spiccato bowing
  - " III: double stops in octaves
  - " VI: double stops
  - " VIII: double, triple, and quadruple stops
  - " IX: pizzicato
  - " X: harmonics

### *Violins in the orchestra*

Saint-Saëns: *Danse Macabre* (with solo violin obvious at times)
Sibelius: *Valse Triste* (muted)
Beethoven: *Symphony No.* 3, second movement (opening strain in low register)

Prokofiev: *Classical Symphony*, second movement (high register)
Mendelssohn: *Midsummer Night's Dream Overture* (after four opening chords on woodwinds)
Wagner: *Prelude* to first act of *Lohengrin* (each violin part divided for complete harmony in violins)
Ippolitov-Ivanov: *March of the Sardar* from *Caucasian Sketches* (after piccolo solo)

*Viola as a solo instrument*

Any solo recording by William Primrose
Berlioz: *Harold in Italy*, first and third movements
Hindemith: *Trauermusik* for viola and orchestra
Ippolitov-Ivanov: *In the Village*, from *Caucasian Sketches* (viola and English horn have dialogue, contrasting the timbre of this string with the woodwind of similar range)

*Violas in the orchestra*

Berlioz: *Roman Carnival Overture* (after a short introduction, the English horn plays a slow melody, which is taken up by the violas)

*'Cello as a solo instrument*

Any 'cello concerto or independent solo by such performers as Pablo Casals, Emanuel Feuermann, Gregor Piatigorsky, Leonard Rose

*'Cellos in the orchestra*

Villa-Lobos: *Bachianas Brasileiras No. 5* (eight 'cellos, with soprano)
Brahms: *Symphony No. 2*, first movement (third theme)
Brahms: *Symphony No. 2*, second movement (first theme)
Tchaikovsky: *Symphony No. 6*, second movement (beginning)
Schubert: *Symphony No. 8*, first movement (second theme)
Beethoven: *Symphony No. 5*, second movement (beginning: unison with violas)
Beethoven: *Symphony No. 5*, third movement (beginning: unison with basses)

*Bass as a solo instrument*

Saint-Saëns: *Carnival of the Animals: Elephants*

*Basses in the orchestra*

Schubert: *Symphony No. 8,* first movement: introduction (an octave below the 'cellos)
Beethoven: *Symphony No. 5,* third movement: beginning and again midway (an octave below the 'cellos)
Prokofiev: *Classical Symphony,* second movement: second part, pizzicato (doubling with bassoon)

*Harp*

Ravel: *Introduction and Allegro for Harp, Flute, Clarinet and String Quartet*
Tchaikovsky: *Nutcracker Suite: Waltz of the Flowers*
Franck: *Symphony in D minor,* second movement (with pizzicato strings)
Debussy: *Danses Sacrée et Profane*
Dello Joio: *Concerto for Harp and Orchestra,* second movement

*Piano trio*

Beethoven: *Archduke Trio*
Schubert: *Trio No. 1 in B-flat*
Brahms: *Trio No. 1 in B major*

*String quartet*

Dvořák: *Quartet No. 6 in F major,* "American"
Tchaikovsky: *Quartet in D major,* No. 1
Mozart: *Quartet No. 15 in D minor* (K.421)
Haydn: *Quartet in C major,* "Emperor"
Beethoven: *Quartet No. 13 in B-flat,* Op. 130
Other quartets by the above, and by Bartók, Borodin, Brahms, Schubert, and Smetana

*String choir and string orchestra*

Tchaikovsky: *Serenade for Strings*
Mozart: *Eine Kleine Nachtmusik*
Grieg: *Ase's Death,* from *Peer Gynt Suite*
Barber: *Adagio for Strings*
Bach: *Brandenburg Concerto No. 3*

*Special treatment of string choir in full orchestrations*

Tchaikovsky: *Symphony No. 4,* third movement (strings pizzicato throughout)

Tchaikovsky: *Nutcracker Suite: Danse Arabe* (strings muted throughout)

Grieg: *Anitra's Dance,* from *Peer Gynt Suite* (strings pizzicato)

Franck: *Symphony in D minor,* second movement (strings pizzicato, with harp, in first portion)

Pierné: *Entrance of the Little Fauns* from *Cydalise* (lower strings pizzicato, upper strings col legno)

Dvořák: *From the New World Symphony,* second movement (strings muted)

## The Woodwind Choir

In the symphony orchestra the woodwind choir is second in importance to the string choir. There are two reasons for this: (1) a wider variety of orchestra tone coloring is obtainable from the woodwinds than from either the brasses or the percussion instruments; and (2) examination of orchestra scores will show that the woodwinds are used more than are any other instruments except the strings (with the possible exception of one brass and one percussion: the French horn and the timpani).

All woodwinds have the same basic acoustical arrangement, although both the method of setting up the vibrating column of air and the manipulation of this column for changes in pitch will vary somewhat among the different instruments.

The basic range of each instrument depends upon the length of the tubing, from the small piccolo to the large and cumbersome contrabassoon. The longer the air column provided by the tube length, the lower the sound will be. The lowest note possible on each instrument is produced when the fingers of the performer are so placed on the holes and keys of the mechanism that they close all openings between the extremes of the instrument, mak-

# *Orchestral Instruments*

*STRING ORCHESTRA*

*STRING QUARTET*

*STRING BASS SECTION*

*THE HARP*

*THE HARP MECHANISM*

*THE HARP PEDALS*

*WOODWIND QUINTET*

*"NO REED" INSTRUMENTS*

*DOUBLE REED INSTRUMENTS*

*TROMBONE AND BASS TROMBONE*

*STRING ORCHESTRA in rehearsal (above)*

*STRING QUARTET (top, right). Note the relative size of the viola, r., as compared to the violins.*

*STRING BASS SECTION (bottom, right)*

THE HARP *(above)*

THE HARP MECHANISM *controlled by the pedals (top, right)*

THE HARP PEDALS *(bottom, right). The instrument is now set in the key of four flats.*

*WOODWIND QUINTET (above): l. to r.: flute, bassoon, French horn, clarinet, oboe*

*"NO REED" INSTRUMENTS (top, left): flutes and piccolo*

*DOUBLE REED INSTRUMENTS (bottom, left): oboes and English horn, front; bassoons in rear*

*TROMBONE AND BASS TROMBONE*

ing the entire length of the instrument the vibrating body. As various fingers are removed holes are opened, thus shortening the length of the vibrating column with resultant higher tones. This fundamental method of changing the pitch is used for the low and middle registers on all woodwind instruments; the very high tones get into the field of overblowing and the use of harmonics, which is rather involved and not necessary for inclusion here.

Like the strings, the woodwinds may be subdivided on the basis of the method of producing the vibrations that cause the sound. Tones are produced by the use of a single reed, a double reed, or no reed at all, in which case the vibration is caused by blowing across an open hole. According to these divisions the woodwind choir in the symphony orchestra contains the following, with the number of each listed:

| | | |
|---|---|---|
| "No reeds" | | 3 |
| flutes, piccolo | 3 | |
| Single reeds | | 3 |
| clarinets, bass clarinet | 3 | |
| Double reeds | | 6 |
| oboes, English horn | 3 | |
| bassoons, contrabassoon | 3 | |
| | | 12 |

Note that the twelve performers are divided into four groups of three each, and that each grouping of three includes two instruments. In each case these two instruments are either technically identical or differ only slightly in their performance, but are of different sizes. By having these groupings, each of which includes a main instrument and its secondary, or "doubling" instrument which can be handled equally well by the performer on the main instrument, it is possible to take care of the variations in scoring the composers have made to get the effects they desire. For instance, in the "no-reed" group most music calls for only two performers, but often three are used. The following combinations of flute and piccolo have been called for in orchestrations, which shows the necessity of having three performers capable of playing both the flute and the piccolo:

| | |
|---|---|
| 1 flute | 2 piccolos |
| 2 flutes | 1 flute and 1 piccolo |
| 3 flutes | 2 flutes and 1 piccolo |
| 1 piccolo | 1 flute and 2 piccolos |

Generally, if all three performers are needed by the demands of the score, the combination of two flutes and one piccolo will be called for; this is also true of the other groupings giving the additional normal full personnel of two clarinets and one bass clarinet, two oboes and one English horn, two bassoons and one contrabassoon.

## THE "NO-REED" INSTRUMENTS

### THE FLUTE

The *flute* has an ancient background, being the ultimate instrument of the *flauto traverso* group which uses the principle of air blown across a hole in the side of the instrument as versus the *flute-a-beck* group wherein the air was blown directly into the top end. The principle of starting a vibrating column of air to produce a tone without the use of a reed can be demonstrated in several homely ways: (1) by blowing across the neck of an empty or partially filled bottle, and (2) by blowing into your own cupped hands.

The earlier instruments of this type were made of wood, with the air hole near one end and a series of finger holes along the side, these to be so manipulated by the fingers that various pitches could be sounded. The nearest modern counterpart is the fife, which unadorned by side keys as it is, can play the notes of only one scale, and is therefore limited in its usage to playing with drums and with other fifes. As the instrument developed, other holes were bored into the wood to produce the chromatic tones, but since the human hands did not have enough fingers to cover all of these holes they were stopped by padded keys and mechanisms which were manipulated by the fingers available when such a chromatic tone was desired. In order to make this system of fingering most convenient to the player and at the same time permit the most fluency, experimenters worked out over three hundred different fingering systems. The variation that proved best is known as the Boehm system, named for its inventor Theobald Boehm who was the most enterprising of the innovators, and who introduced his system well over a hundred years ago.

Changes have also taken place in the material used. As the wooden instrument was susceptible to cracking due to changes in temperature and moisture, it was replaced by metal. A silver alloy is generally used, but some famous flautists have had instruments built for them in silver, gold, and even platinum. Therefore, although the metal appearance of the flute might seem to contradict its presence in the woodwind family, it still belongs there because of its genesis and the physics involved in its performance.

The flute is a soprano instrument, its lowest sounding note corresponding to middle C on the piano. In comparison with the soprano voices the flute can also be classified as a coloratura instrument that can also be used in a lyrical way just as a coloratura soprano can sing lyric songs. But its coloratura possibilities are so great that composers favor its use even in duets with coloratura sopranos. Its flexibility of performance also makes it the instrument chosen to imitate the singing of birds when such trills and warblings are desired by the composer.

### THE PICCOLO

The *piccolo* is simply a small flute, half the size of the larger instrument, and therefore, because of the physical ratio of the length of the tubing of the two, one octave higher in sound. In fact, the full and correct name for the instrument is variously *flauto piccolo, petite flûte* and *Kleine Flöte* in Italian, French, and German, all three being literally translated as "small flute." But here again, as in the case of the 'cello, we have become careless and speak of the instrument as a *piccolo* or a "small," not bothering to designate what particular small thing we have in mind.

The piccolo is not used nearly as much as is the flute; when it is scored for, it has one of two usages: (1) to utilize the brilliance and shrillness of its particular timbre, or (2) to add higher notes to, and thus extend the upper range of, the orchestra for balance when the full ensemble is playing. It has been termed the "imp of the orchestra," which is not bad nomenclature since its color can be extremely impish in character.[6]

## THE SINGLE-REED INSTRUMENTS

### THE CLARINET

If you hold a piece of coarse grass between your thumbs and blow on it in a certain way, you can produce a shrill sound; the

[6] In listening to actual performances of musical organizations you will have more opportunity to listen to the piccolo in band music than you will in orchestral compositions, for it is given much more to do in band music, particularly in marches.

air chamber formed by the hands is not large enough to make this sound very musical. In like manner, if you attach a piece of reed (which is cane and therefore related to the grass) to a mouthpiece and blow it, you get a similar sound. But if you attach this mouthpiece to a clarinet, you have added a length of tubing sufficient to give control to the reed vibration, and to produce musical tones. Another homely method of utilizing the single reed principle of tone production is to be found in the harmonica where blowing into a single hole will cause a small metal "reed" to vibrate at a rate that produces a desired tone.

Although the *clarinet* was accepted as a regular member of the symphony orchestra at a later date than were the flute, the oboe, and the bassoon, it has become the most popular and most useful of all woodwinds. Its use in the orchestra is based on the fact that (1) it is as capable of performing coloratura passages as is the flute; (2) it can be given lyric passages with success; (3) it has a dramatic quality, particularly in its lower register. It also has a greater range than the other comparatively high woodwinds, starting with a low note almost an octave below that of the flute and soaring up into the high reaches of that instrument. Its popularity is due to the fact that it is a good triple-threat instrument: in addition to its importance in the symphony orchestra it is the most important instrument of the woodwind choir of the band, and is used in greater numbers than any other instrument in that organization. It is also, with the saxophones, the mainstay of the woodwind section of the dance orchestra.

Although the clarinet is made of either wood or metal, orchestra players in particular prefer the wooden instrument both because of its tone quality and because of the feel of the instrument in playing it. The fact that two different clarinets built in the keys of B flat and A are called for by composers of orchestra music should be known. However, since they are identical in technique and in usage and are practically identical in size and timbre, it is not necessary to think of them as different.[7]

### THE BASS CLARINET

The clarinets mentioned above are actually the sopranos of a large family of such instruments, all fingered the same way, but built in nine different sizes to produce the clarinet tone in different ranges. Many of these are used in the band, but in the orchestra the traditional doubling instrument is the *bass clarinet.* Since the tubing is twice the length of the clarinet tubing, the bass clarinet is built with a curved metal neck and a curved-up saxophone-like bell at the bottom for ease in handling. Because of this doubled length of the air column the bass clarinet, which is built in B flat, sounds one octave lower than notes fingered in a similar way on the *B-flat clarinet.*

Although it is sometimes used in ensemble music to fill in the lower notes of the harmony, the chief use of the bass clarinet is to extend the clarinet range downward, so that solo passages with the clarinet timbre can be written below the range possible on the higher instrument. In comparison with the regular clarinets it is not very much used.

## THE DOUBLE-REED INSTRUMENTS

The difficulty of creating a sound by the use of a double reed can be approximated by pinching a soda-fountain straw at one end so that the sides are almost together, then blowing through this end. After some experimenting it might be possible to produce a squawking sound. The double-reed player has somewhat

[7] The reason for the two is simply a matter of ease of performance depending on the key signature of the composition.

the same trouble getting his reed to sound, particularly if he is a beginner; this control of the reed helps to make instruments of the double-reed family relatively difficult to play.

It might be wise at this point to contradict the popular but erroneous idea that continued performance on a double-reed instrument will ultimately affect the mental stability of the performer. Many oboe and bassoon players have been performers for thirty or forty years with no such results; we know of no authentic case to substantiate the misconception.[8]

Since these instruments are both difficult and expensive, for many years they were played only by professional performers. It is a healthy sign that more and more high-school students are learning to play double reeds, because there is a realization that no matter how competent the other performers in a band or orchestra may be, the absence of the peculiar timbre of the various double reeds will be noticeable in the over-all effect.

### THE OBOE

In the double-reed group there are two major instruments, each with its doubling instrument, which gives us as many different double reeds as there are other woodwinds combined. The *oboe* is the highest of this group, with its low note just one tone below that of the flute, but with not as high a range. It is largely a lyric instrument and does not lend itself to coloratura performance. The timbre is reedy and nasal, and capable of much greater penetration than the size of the instrument would suggest. Its oriental background makes it useful for oriental coloring; its rural antecedents make it a choice in giving a pastoral effect.

[8] Some other instrumental performers claim that it works the other way, and that "you have to be slightly nuts before you'll try to learn to play one of those things," but this is just as mistaken an idea.

Unlike the flute and clarinet which have cylindrical bores, the oboe has a slightly conical bore; the reed is inserted in the end of the instrument without benefit of a mouthpiece.

The derivation of the word *oboe* is interesting. The instrument was developed by the French and was called by them the *hautbois*, a term literally translated as "high wood" and still used as the French name of the instrument. The Italians came as close as possible to the French word by the phonetic spelling *oboe*, pronounced in three syllables. We, in turn, use the Italian spelling with an Anglicized pronunciation.

### THE ENGLISH HORN

The doubling instrument of the oboe which in reality is an alto oboe is the *English horn*. Half again the size of the oboe, it sounds five notes deeper in range, which is similar to the pitch relationship between the violin and the viola. The English horn differs slightly from the oboe shape in two respects: (1) the reed is placed on a metal tube made with a slight angle, this tube being inserted in the upper end of the instrument for performance facility; (2) the open end is shaped somewhat like an inverted electric light bulb, which makes the tone a bit more subdued and less penetrating than the oboe tone.

As every book or lecture about the English horn will remind you, the name is a complete misnomer, since the instrument is a woodwind developed in France. No explanation for the term has been authenticated, but the following seems to be the most logical. In every language the word *horn* (French: *cor*) is used as a generality for all instruments that are blown. A French instrumentalist, attempting to make a more playable alto oboe, discovered that by using the metal pipe with its angle between the main body of the instrument and the reed he had an instrument that could be held and played in a more comfortable position. He probably told a journalistic friend about his new *angle horn*, or *cor anglé*, in a sort of slang way. Since *anglé* (angled) and *Anglais* (English) have the same pronunciation in French it is quite probable that through misunderstanding the newly developed instrument broke into print as a *cor Anglais*, or *English horn*.

The English horn, being of comparatively recent development, is a late addition to the symphony orchestra. Even now it is not used extensively in ensembles, but is scored for when its plaintive timbre will take the spotlight in a solo passage.

### THE BASSOON

When the Italians named this instrument a *fagotto* (bundle of sticks), they weren't far from wrong in a descriptive way. The *bassoon* is an awkward instrument to play and even to assemble, since it comes in five sections in addition to the reed. It has an extensive range from bass through baritone to high tenor; its low note is one tone below the lowest string of the 'cello. Within this range it has a variety of timbres, the two extremes differing as much as or more than on any other single instrument. The bass tones have almost a froglike croak; the beauty increases in the middle register and then approaches a thin, whiny tone in the upper extreme. These descriptions do not sound very complimentary, and yet the instruments and bassoonists as well command great respect. It must be admitted that the name "clown of the orchestra" often applied to the bassoon suits quite well, for there are certain passages in very serious works which, even in the hands of a skilled performer are likely to sound somewhat comic.

### THE CONTRABASSOON

The *contrabassoon*, which is the doubling instrument in the bassoon group, has twice the length of tubing of the bassoon, which gives it a tone range one octave lower. It is capable of playing the lowest notes in the entire orchestral gamut and consequently, when used, which is seldom, it adds depth to the complete orchestra range. Only rarely does it perform in a passage where it can be distinguished as the predominating instrument.

### WOODWINDS IN COMBINATION

There is little recorded material for combinations of woodwinds alone, for there is not very much literature for such groups in comparison to that written for the various string ensembles. Recently, more published material for woodwind groups is coming on the market; this is probably because music educators are demanding additional material to use both for study and for public performance for their good woodwind players. The one standard woodwind ensemble of long standing is known as the *woodwind quintet*; it is composed of a flute, an oboe, a clarinet, and a bassoon, with a French horn as the fifth instrument. This may seem a bit like cheating on terminology, but the French horn blends so well with the actual woodwinds that it has been traditionally included in the ensemble even though it is a brass instrument, and no one seems to be very much worried by its presence there.

## *SUGGESTED LISTENING*

### *Flute*

Mozart: *Flute Concerto No. 1*
Griffes: *Poem for Flute and Orchestra*
Tchaikovsky: *Danse Chinoise,* from *Nutcracker Suite*
Saint-Saëns: *Birds,* from the *Carnival of the Animals*
Prokofiev: *Peter and the Wolf* (the Bird theme)
Tchaikovsky: *Dance of the Toy Flutes,* from *Nutcracker Suite* (three flutes)

Donizetti: The Mad Scene, from *Lucia di Lammermoor* (flute with coloratura soprano)
Music for the Flute. Six selections played by William Kincaid

*Piccolo*

Ravel: *Laideronette, Empress of the Pagoda,* from *Mother Goose Suite* (after a short introduction)
Ippolitov-Ivanov: *March of the Sardar,* from *Caucasian Sketches* (first melody)
Pierné: *Entrance of the Little Fauns,* from *Cydalise* (impudent flights above trumpet solo)
Tchaikovsky: *Symphony No. 4,* third movement (in the woodwind choir portion, and two short flights above the brasses)
Sousa: *Stars and Stripes Forever*

*Clarinet*

Hindemith: *Sonata for Clarinet and Piano*
Weber: *Concertino for Clarinet*
Copland: *Concerto for Clarinet and String Orchestra*
Debussy: *Rhapsody No. 1 for Clarinet*
Brahms: *Quintet for Clarinet and Strings*
Saint-Saëns: *Fossils,* from *Carnival of the Animals*
Stravinsky: *Three Pieces for Solo Clarinet*
Prokofiev: *Peter and the Wolf* (the Cat theme)

*Bass clarinet*

Grofé: *On the Trail,* from *Grand Canyon Suite* (continuation of downward run on oboe)
Tchaikovsky: *Dance of the Sugar Plum Fairy,* from *Nutcracker Suite* (several short countermelodies toward the start of the celeste solo)

*Oboe*

Handel: *Concerto No. 3 in G minor for Oboe and Strings*
Mozart: *Quartet in F major for Oboe and Strings*
Grofé: *On the Trail,* from *Grand Canyon Suite* (after violin cadenza)
Berlioz: *Symphonie Fantastique,* third movement (dialogue with English horn)

Ippolitov-Ivanov: *In the Village,* from *Caucasian Sketches* (after dialogue between viola and English horn)
Saint-Saëns: *Bacchanale,* from *Samson et Dalila*
Prokofiev: *Peter and the Wolf* (the Duck theme)

*English horn*

Berlioz: *Roman Carnival Overture* (slow melody after fast introduction)
Sibelius: *Swan of Tuonela*
Franck: *Symphony in D minor,* second movement
Dvořák: *From the New World Symphony,* second movement
Berlioz: *Symphonie Fantastique,* third movement (dialogue with oboe)
Ippolitov-Ivanov: *In the Village,* from *Caucasian Sketches* (dialogue with viola)

*Bassoon*

Poulenc: *Trio for Clarinet, Bassoon, and Piano*
Mozart: *Bassoon Concerto No. 1 in B-flat major*
Phillips: *Concert Piece for Bassoon and Strings*
Dukas: *Sorcerer's Apprentice* (original melody following introduction)
Tchaikovsky: *Symphony No. 6,* fourth movement (introduction)
Prokofiev: *Peter and the Wolf* (The Grandfather theme)
Prokofiev: *Classical Symphony,* second movement (with pizzicato basses)

*Contrabassoon*

Ravel: *Beauty and the Beast,* from *Mother Goose Suite* (after the clarinet solo there are two short solo passages, followed by countermelody)

*Woodwind quintet*

Bartoš: *Incidental Music to Le Bourgeois Gentilhomme*
Nielsen: *Quintet for Wind Instruments*
Schultz: *Une Amourette*

*Woodwind choir in the orchestra*

Tchaikovsky: *Symphony No. 4,* third movement (after pizzicato strings)

Mussorgsky: from *Pictures at an Exhibition: Tuileries* (throughout, except for few strings toward end)
Mussorgsky: second *Promenade,* following *Gnomes* (after horn melody)
Mussorgsky: *Ballet of the Unhatched Chicks* (with addition of a few strings pizzicato)
Mussorgsky: *The Great Gate at Kiev* (after brass and full orchestra; again after full orchestra)

## *The Brass Choir*

It is not necessary to subdivide the instruments of the brass choir since the method of tone production is the same for all of them: the vibration of the lips of the performer plus the addition of an output of air from the lungs sets in motion the air chamber of the instrument, causing the musical tone. Once the tone has been started, changes in pitch are made in a variety of ways, but this compares to the techniques of changing the pitch on the woodwinds and strings.

The brass instruments used in the symphony orchestra are:

| | |
|---|---|
| trumpets | 4 |
| French horns | 4 |
| trombones | 3 |
| tuba | 1 |
| | 12 |

As in the case of the woodwinds there are twelve performers, but in the brass choir they are divided into three groups of four players each, based on relative pitch relationships. There is a high quartet of trumpets, a middle-range quartet of French horns, and a low-range quartet of three trombones plus the lower tuba.

### THE TRUMPET

Serving as the heroic soprano of the symphony orchestra, the *trumpet* is one of the best-known and most easily recognized instruments. This is explained to some degree by the presence of the trumpet in the dance band, and its importance with its companion, the cornet, in the military band. It can be, and in much modern music often is, muted, causing not only a softer tone, but one with a timbre slightly different from that of the open instrument, and it is called upon to play softly at times. But its chief use is the one that brings out the power and resonance of the instrument when blown with full breath and with no attempt to conceal its identity.

Certain pitches, similar to those on the valveless bugle, are made by changes in the rapidity of the lip vibrations. These tones, which belong to the harmonic series of overtones of the instrument, are basic; intermediate tones are produced by changing the length of the resonating tube by the use of the three piston valves. To call the valves by their usual designation of 1st, 2nd, and 3rd is confusing; instead think of them as valves A, B, and C, and assign a comparative weighting to them of 2, 1, and 3, in that order. The B valve has the shortest amount of additional tubing; the A valve has twice as much as B; the C valve has a length equal to the sum of A plus B. With this in mind we can start at any lip position, without the use of valves, which produces a given tone, and by adding additional tubing lengths that grow gradually longer we can create all the possible tones. This is shown in the following table:

| LIP TONE | ADDITIONAL TUBING | NEW PITCH |
|---|---|---|
| G | valve B (1) | G flat |
| G | valve A (2) | F natural |
| G | valves A and B (1 plus 2 = 3) | E natural |
| G | valves B and C (1 plus 3 = 4) | E flat |
| G | valves A and C (2 plus 3 = 5) | D natural |
| G | valves A, B, and C (2 plus 1 plus 3 = 6) | D flat |

Now that all the additional tubing has been added by the use of all three valves simultaneously, there can be no lower tone made in this series. The lips are now used with a looser vibration, and the next lower note, C, will sound. The same system of fingering will lower this tone by half steps as noted above.

Four trumpets have been listed for the orchestra, even though two are enough to handle much of the music written for this medium. However, it is advisable to have both a third and a fourth trumpet available for those compositions that call for the full complement.

### THE FRENCH HORN

The *French horn* is the most important brass choir instrument of the orchestra; in fact, it is one of the most important instruments of the whole orchestra without regard to its choir, and normally plays about as much of the time as any instrument, because of its adaptability. It can be played with a brassy tone, fitting in with the rest of its choir, but it is normally comparatively mellow and therefore serves equally well with the woodwinds or the strings. As such, it is the best combining instrument in the entire ensemble, being used with any choir or with any combination of choirs.

If a professional performer tells you he plays a *horn,* don't make the mistake of asking him which one, for here is one case where we add to the foreign name of the instrument rather than use an abbreviated form as we have in several other instances. The German *Horn,* the French *cor,* and the Italian *corno* all suffice in these other countries, but we carefully add a word, and use *French horn* for our designation. The professional simply uses the European tradition and speaks of the instrument as the *horn.*

Technically, the horn differs from the other valve instruments of the brass choir in several ways: (1) its mouthpiece is cone-shaped rather than cupped; (2) its valves work on the rotary rather than the piston principle; (3) it is the only instrument played with the left hand, the right hand being encased in the bell where it is used for muting and other effects; (4) it is so built that it utilizes the middle and higher overtones rather than the fundamental tone, with consequent difficulty in the more sensitive lip adjustments required.

For its incomparable use in solo passages of subdued lyrical tone color the horn has been rightfully given the sobriquet of "poet of the orchestra." Its solos will be either purely lyrical in character, or perhaps dramatic if it is played in imitation of its predecessor, the hunting horn.

Historically, the French horn has been built in many different keys, with correspondingly different sizes. At the present time the horn built in F is the standard instrument used; the *double horn,* which has additional optional tubing that can be used to change the basic key, is becoming very popular, but for our purposes of recognition we can safely think of just one instrument known as the French horn.

### THE TROMBONE

The lower range of the brasses is dominated by the noble tone of the *trombone.* The technique of playing this instrument is the most obvious of all, for starting with any given lip position the pitch is lowered as the telescopic slide is drawn out in units of about three inches. This is possible in six consecutive positions in addition to the closed position of the slide; these positions change the pitch of the note by lengthening the air column in the tube as described above in the case of the valves on the trumpet.

Like the trumpet the trombone is well known by sight, because of its use in the dance orchestra and in the marching band where it usually appears in the front rank for obvious reasons. You should be cautioned not to try to recognize trombone timbre by listening to the dance orchestras that feature them, because in many cases the dance trombonist seems to take a delight in making his instrument sound as unlike the true trombone as possible.

When the three trombones are used in professional symphony orchestras, #3 and often #2 are *bass trombones,* which differ from the instrument we are used to observing, by (1) an additional bit of tubing near the upper end that may be used by pressing a hidden thumb valve; and (2) a slightly larger bore throughout. The additional tubing permits the playing of several notes below the low tone of the common, or tenor, trombone; the larger bore produces a tone quality that is slightly different on the side of bigness. But again, as in the case of the single and double horns, there is no reason to try to differentiate between the two by ear. Either one may be considered as the typical trombone.

The one technique that is peculiar to the trombone because of its slide mechanism is the well-known *glissando* effect. This has been utilized by composers in marches written to display the technique peculiar to the instrument; it is also used by performers in the jazz field. It is used sparingly in symphonic music. The muting of the trombone by the insertion of a material cone in the bell is also used sparingly in orchestra music, but appears more frequently in music written for the concert band and the dance orchestra.

### THE TUBA

To complete the quartet of low brasses a *tuba* is added to the three trombones. This instrument is lower than the trombones, and gives a good basic note when the four are used as a quartet in choralelike music. The *tuba* (here used instead of the term *bass* to avoid confusion with the *string bass*) is built in a variety of sizes and shapes: the variation preferred for use in the orchestra is the upright instrument, built compactly and held on the lap of the performer.

In orchestra music the tuba is seldom given a passage by itself but is generally used in combination with the other brasses, or, if used when the full orchestra is playing, its function is to add to the basic tone already being produced by the string bass section in loud passages.

### BRASSES IN COMBINATION

What literature there is for the brasses in combination, such as trumpet trios, brass quartets, and brass sextets, has stemmed largely from the band rather than the orchestral use of these instruments; as such there are not many good recordings available. However, in orchestra music it is not uncommon to find passages wherein various brasses are used in combination, with the other instruments temporarily silent.

## *SUGGESTED LISTENING*

### *Trumpet*

Verdi: *Grand March*, from *Aïda*
Purcell: *Trumpet Voluntary*
Mussorgsky: *Promenade, from Pictures at an Exhibition* (opening measures)
Mussorgsky: *Samuel Goldenberg and Schmuyle* (rhythmic figure after introduction)
Pierné: *Entrance of the Little Fauns*, from *Cydalise* (muted)
Handel: *The Trumpet Shall Sound*, from the *Messiah* (with bass voice)

### *French horn*

Mozart: *Concerto No. 3 for Horn in E-flat major*
Mendelssohn: *Nocturne*, from *Midsummer Night's Dream*

Weber: *Overture to Der Freischütz* (after introduction)
Tchaikovsky: *Symphony No.* 5, second movement (after introduction)
Strauss: *Till Eulenspiegel* (solos near beginning taking in almost entire range of the instrument)
Beethoven: *Symphony No.* 3, third movement (middle section)

### *Trombone*

Rimsky-Korsakov: *Concerto for Trombone and Band*
Rimsky-Korsakov: *Russian Easter Overture* (after introduction, and halfway through record, in recitative)
Berlioz: *Roman Carnival Overture* (midway in recording)
Grofé: *On the Trail*, from *Grand Canyon Suite* (slow-moving solo after second oboe-bass clarinet run)

### *Brass choir in the orchestra*

Mussorgsky: *Promenade*, from *Pictures at an Exhibition* (after trumpet introduction)
Mussorgsky: *Catacombs* from *Pictures at an Exhibition*
Mussorgsky: *The Great Gate at Kiev*, from *Pictures at an Exhibition* (opening theme, with timpani)
Tchaikovsky: *Symphony No.* 4, third movement (after string and woodwind sections)

## *The Percussion Choir*

If we were to try to divide the percussion instruments into groups according to the method of setting up the tone as was done with the strings and the woodwinds, we would end up with no division at all, for the word *percussion* means that the tone is produced by striking the instrument. If the striking agent or the type of surface struck were used as a basis, we might have almost as many subdivisions as there are instruments. However, some basis of division into groups is desirable because of the large number of different instruments in the percussion choir. The most logical subdivision into two groups is on the basis of the intonation.

Instruments of *definite pitch*
- timpani
- bells
- chimes
- celeste
- xylophone
- etc.

Instruments of *indefinite pitch*
- snare drum
- bass drum
- cymbals
- gong
- triangle
- tom-tom
- tambourine
- castanets
- etc.

You will no doubt notice two ways in which this list differs from those used for the other choirs. First, there is the omission of the numbers of each instrument in the orchestra, because this is too variable. It is sufficient to know that there is one performer for the timpani, and that generally two other percussionists can take care of whatever else is called for by the composer. Sometimes several more players are pressed into service, and one composition requires sixteen percussion players!

The second item that may have been noticed is the fact that listed under both subheadings is an "etc." These are important parts of the lists, for in order to get special effects composers have been utilizing all sorts of materials that will give forth a sound when struck, such as coconut shells, woodblocks, wash boilers, sheets of corrugated iron, and other things equally far away from the general conception of orchestra instruments. In addition, the recent trend toward more North American performances of South American music has given us a number of native instruments from our friends to the south: maracas, claves, bongos, Congo drums, gourds, timbales, and again "etc."

## PERCUSSION INSTRUMENTS OF DEFINITE PITCH

### THE TIMPANI

For our convenience the percussion instruments are divided into (1) those of definite intonation that actually add to the sum total of the music through their ability to produce musical sounds of different pitches, and (2) those with no definite pitch (or, as in the case of the triangle, one pitch only) that are used for coloring effects. Only one of the entire choir is scored for in practically all compositions; the others may or may not be used, and generally are not.

The important percussion instrument is the *timpani;* it is played by an individual who has made timpani performance his sole specialization: he would no more stoop to playing other percussions in the orchestra than a steam shovel operator in a large excavation job would deign to use a hand shovel or drive a truck. He is the aristocrat of the percussionists, and if he has a flair for showmanship he probably gets more attention from the audience than anyone else on stage with the possible exception of the conductor.

The word *timpani* has been used as a singular noun, designating it as a single instrument, whereas in reality it is a set of instruments. The performer plays on two or even three or four separate drums that are similar except in size. The word *kettledrums,* which is another perfectly correct name for these instruments, suggests their shape. They are bowl-shaped drums made of copper or brass, with a head, or playing surface, stretched across the open top. The instruments are usually played with soft headed mallets, although for thunderous effects the composer might call for harder mallets to be used.

The earlier timpani were tuned by manipulating a set of hand screws around the upper rim of the instrument, which, being a rather slow and laborious process, meant that the two drums were usually pretuned to the two most important notes of the scale (*do* and *so*) and remained in that tuning during the entire composition, or were changed only if there was a long period of rest for the timpanist. A more recent invention has given us almost instantaneous changes in tuning by the use of a pedal device. This, in turn, has increased the scope of the instruments; modern music is full of examples in which different notes are played quite rapidly on either or both of the instruments, to the extent of playing actual tunes.

Each drum has a range of slightly over half an octave so that when two of different sizes are used it is possible to get all the chromatic tones of a complete scale of an octave in the playing range.

### THE BELLS

The remaining instruments of the percussion choir to be discussed are very seldom used in orchestra music. Each one has a particular timbre, and each one suggests one or more special effects. Fortunately, they are generally saved for the time when these effects are wanted; otherwise their use could become very monotonous.

The *bells,* which are almost as well known by their German name *Glockenspiel,* are a set of bars made of bell metal, of graduated sizes and placed on a frame in two series that are similar to the white and black keys of the piano keyboard. Struck by hard rubber or wooden mallets, they produce what can only be described as high bell-like tones. Their particular use is to give the effect of the notes of a small clock, or to add color to a melody that is being played by the violins or some other instrument.

### THE CHIMES

The *chimes* are a graduated series of metal tubes suspended from a frame, and struck with a wooden or hard leather-covered hammer. Their tone, which is much deeper than that of the orchestra bells, is chiefly used in imitation of the tower bells of a church.

### THE CELESTE

The *celeste* was invented comparatively recently in order to be able to produce the tones of the orchestra bells in multiple tones rather than as a single melody line. The instrument looks like the case of a small portable piano, with a four-octave keyboard similar to that of the piano. Using piano technique, the performer compresses a key which in turn strikes a bell-metal bar. Because piano technique is used in performance, the celeste is often given a passage to play while the other instruments are silent; or it may be used to embellish the music being played by other instruments. Although seldom used with the symphony orchestra, it has appeared as a member of some of the large dance-concert orchestras with interesting results.

### THE XYLOPHONE

The *xylophone* consists of a graduated series of wooden bars suspended on a frame in two rows representing the white and black keys of the piano. Performance generally calls for hard mallets, for as far as symphonic music is concerned the use is limited to those compositions that want to utilize the wooden tone produced to represent some particular sound such as the rattling of skeleton bones.[9]

[9] The same instrument and its closely allied percussion, the marimba, are more widely used for entertainment purposes. Used in this manner, the per-

## PERCUSSION INSTRUMENTS OF INDEFINITE PITCH

The sound-producers considered in this group are more logically band instruments, and the performer who plays them will have much more enjoyment in the band than he will in the orchestra. In the latter case he might go through an entire concert season without being called upon to strike a single note. This is possible but hardly probable, for whereas the earlier orchestra music, which still makes up a considerable part of our programs, was written with timpani as the sole percussion instrument, more recent music has utilized the percussive color to a greater degree. When his talent is used, the percussionist is generally called on to perform in a manner that will leave no doubt in the minds of the listeners of his intentions or those of the composer.

### THE SNARE DRUM

The *snare drum* of the orchestra is similar to the same but better-known instrument of the band, except that it is built with less depth, which gives it a more refined tone quality. This is obviously desirable since it is used to give a martial color to the music and not for actual marching in the great outdoors as is its band counterpart. The drum has two heads stretched in a frame: the significant timbre is caused by the lower head and the wire snares stretched across it, which vibrate when the upper head is struck by the wooden drumsticks. In addition to its chief use it may be called upon to emphasize any particular rhythm being used in the composition.

---

formance technique and the resultant sound are quite different from the symphonic use: the music may sound like sustained notes in full harmony, due to the use of soft-headed mallets, the manipulation of four or more of these by one or more players, and the technique of a continuous rapid repetition of strokes, rather than a single stroke.

### THE BASS DRUM

Used by itself or in connection with the snare drum, the larger *bass drum* can add the basic emphasis of any given rhythmic device, as it is struck with a single beater. Or it may be used with or without the timpani to help build up the orchestra to a loud climax. Not very important by itself, it, like the other percussions, is indispensable for certain desired effects.

### THE CYMBALS

Two circular discs when struck together can emphasize the climax of a musical passage better than any other instrument; or with the bass and snare drums the *cymbals* are almost indispensable in march music. While these are the normal usages, there are others. For instance, a very soft tone can be produced by striking one of the pair with a drumstick or beater, thus helping to substantiate the beat or to add subtle emphasis to a note or to a series of notes in soft passages.

### THE GONG

The *gong,* of oriental origin, is a large, circular, metallic plate suspended by a cord and struck with a mallet. While its original response is not as loud as that produced by a strong clash of the cymbals, it has the power to resonate for a much longer time. An additional peculiarity is the fact that after the instrument is struck the volume actually increases rapidly from the initial impact and then gradually softens down until it dies away. As a coloring instrument much used in oriental and Russian music it is an attention-getter without peer.

### THE TRIANGLE

Geometrically built in accordance with its name, the *triangle* is made of a bar of bell metal and is struck with a metallic beater. Its clear, high, tinkling tone is used to add color to a given passage, either by emphasizing the beat in a nice polite way, or by motivating a chord or a passage by the use of the roll, which is accomplished by fluttering the beater rapidly between two sides close to an angle.

### THE TOM-TOM

The *tom-tom* is a drum with a permanent head, valuable in the production of music representative of the American Indian or of certain Asiatic or African peoples. Its timbre is dull and rather colorless, but the lack of a specific brilliance is in this case the chief attribute of the instrument. It is struck by a beater or by the hand or hands. Be careful not to confuse this with the word *tamtam* that you may find printed in foreign scores, for the latter refers to the *gong* that we have discussed.

### THE TAMBOURINE

There is no intention of disrespect in the statement that in one of its best-known roles the *tambourine* serves not only as a musical instrument but as a collection plate as well. And the older generation will remember it as the favorite instrument of the minstrel show. But actually it has a Spanish origin, as suggested by its French name *tambour de Basque* or "drum of the Basque country." In the orchestra it is used chiefly as the rhythmic instrument in music that has the lilt of one of the southern European dances, particularly Spanish.

A small, comparatively flat instrument with a permanent head on one side only, the tambourine gets its characteristic timbre from the metal jingles inserted in pairs in the wooden frame.[10] When the instrument is struck on its drum head by the hand, or

[10] These jingles resemble the metal discs used when putting tarpaper on a roof so that the nails will not tear the paper.

when it is shaken the jingles come in contact with each other causing a light clinking sound.

#### THE CASTANETS

Another instrument used largely in connection with Spanish music is the *castanets.* The name is derived from the Italian *castagnette* which means "a chestnut." The instrument actually resembles a large chestnut which has been sliced down through the middle with the two halves joined together by a cord. The classical method of performance is stock-in-trade of the Spanish dancer who clicks the two halves together by hand manipulation. Since it takes time to get these castanets set in the hand and since the orchestra percussionist must often go rapidly from one instrument to another, the orchestra variant of the instrument has the two halves hinged to a central handle of the same wooden material. This gives a similar effect.

#### THE "ETCETERAS"

Some of the other instruments that may appear in the percussion choir were suggested by "etc." This list is not inclusive and is expanded by the addition of other objects that may be struck to produce a musical sound or a noise desired by the composer. Any such thing is potentially a member of the percussion choir, but could hardly be thought of as a member in very good standing!

## *SUGGESTED LISTENING*

### *Percussion instruments*

Tchaikovsky: *Symphony No. 4,* fourth movement: cymbals, bass drum, timpani
Delibes: *Bell Song,* from *Lakmé*: bells (with coloratura soprano)
Tchaikovsky: *1812 Overture*: chimes (last portion)

Tchaikovsky: *Dance of the Sugar Plum Fairy,* from *Nutcracker Suite*: celeste solo
Saint-Saëns: *Danse Macabre*: xylophone
Saint-Saëns: *Fossils,* from *Carnival of the Animals*: xylophone
Ravel: *Laideronette, Empress of the Pagoda,* from *Mother Goose Suite*: cymbals, celeste, xylophone, gong
Mussorgsky: *The Market Place at Limoges,* from *Pictures at an Exhibition*: snare drum, cymbals, triangle
Mussorgsky: *Catacombs,* from *Pictures at an Exhibition*: gong (at end)
Sousa: *Semper Fidelis*: snare drum
Berlioz: *Symphonie Fantastique,* fourth movement: timpani
Grofé: *Sunset,* from *Grand Canyon Suite*: triangle, bells, timpani, chimes

### *Percussion ensemble*

Varèse: *Ionisation*

## TEST RECORDS FOR INSTRUMENTAL RECOGNITION

(As you listen to any of these records, listen for the first instrument listed, then get ready to recognize the next one, and so on.)

### *Ravel*

*Pavane of the Sleeping Beauty,* from *Mother Goose Suite*
flute
clarinet (over English horn)
flute
violins (muted)

### *Ravel*

*Hop O'My Thumb,* from *Mother Goose Suite*
violins (muted) and oboe
English horn
clarinet (short)
flute (short)

all strings (muted)
English horn
violins (harmonics, giving whistling effect)
'cello
flute
violins (muted)

## *Grofé*

*Sunrise,* from *Grand Canyon Suite*
timpani, violins, then clarinets (in introduction)
piccolo
flute
English horn
flute
English horn
celeste
flute
celeste
violins (bells above and harp accompaniment)
violas and 'cellos
French horns

## *Grofé*

*On the Trail,* from *Grand Canyon Suite*
violin
oboe (backed up by pizzicato strings and coconut shells)
oboe-bass clarinet run
oboe and piccolo (with French horn countermelody)
oboe-bass clarinet run
trombone
trumpets (with violin countermelody)
celeste
oboe-bass clarinet run
timpani

## *Rimsky-Korsakov*

*Scheherazade Suite,* second movement

violin (with harp background)
bassoon (high register)
oboe (with harp)
violins (with 'cellos added an octave lower)
woodwind choir (with pizzicato strings)
'cello, oboe, French horn, oboe (in quick succession)
trombone, trumpet (muted) (twice)
trombone, trumpet (open)
strings pizzicato and clarinet cadenza (three phrases)
trumpet, woodwinds, strings, triangle, leading into:
full orchestra (march rhythm)
strings pizzicato and bassoon cadenza (three phrases)
full orchestra; after harp glissando:
flute (harp and string accompaniment)
French horn (open, then muted with phrase from solo violin between and following)
add 'cellos and basses, clarinets, etc., to full orchestra

## *Wagner*

*Prelude to Act III* of *Lohengrin*
cymbals
French horns
trombones
oboe
flute
violins
clarinet

## *Bach*

*Little G-minor Fugue*
oboe
English horn
bassoon
bass clarinet
violas
basses

violins
trombones and tuba

*Borodin*

*On the Steppes of Central Asia*
violins (high, sustained)
clarinet
French horn
English horn
clarinet
French horns (trombone harmony)
full orchestra
'cellos and English horn
violins
violas and 'cellos
oboe (violin countermelody)
oboe ('cello countermelody)
full orchestra
horns–clarinet–violins (short passages)
English horn–oboe–flute (short passages)
violins–oboe–clarinet (short passages)
solo violin

*Tchaikovsky*

*Symphony No. 4*, second movement
oboe
'cellos
violins
violas and bassoon (unison)
violins and violas (octaves)
violins and 'cellos (octaves)
clarinet and bassoon (octaves)
strings (octaves)
flute, oboe, clarinet (octaves)
woodwinds, strings
violins (woodwind decorations)

violins and 'cellos (octaves)
clarinet—oboe—flute (short passages)
violins (short)
'cellos (high register)
bassoon (high register)
clarinet—bassoon (short passages)

*Brahms*

*Symphony No.* 3, third movement
'cellos (in high register)
violins
flute, oboe, and horn (in octaves)
woodwinds
violins
woodwinds
strings
horns
oboe
bassoons and clarinets
violins (in octaves)

*Brahms*

*Symphony No.* 4, second movement
horns
clarinet (strings pizzicato in accompaniment)
horn
clarinet and bassoon (in octaves)
horn
clarinet
violins
woodwinds
'cellos
violins
violas
horns (short passage)
violins
horns (short passage)

# *Band Instruments... Organ*

*WOODWINDS IN THE BAND*

*SOME SINGLE REED INSTRUMENTS*

*THE SAXOPHONE FAMILY*

*BRASSES IN THE BAND*

*THE SOPRANO BRASSES*

*THE LOW BRASSES*

*PERCUSSIONS IN THE MARCHING BAND*

*SOME SMALL PERCUSSION INSTRUMENTS*

*OTHER PERCUSSION INSTRUMENTS*

*THE CONSOLE OF THE ELECTRIC ORGAN*

*WOODWINDS IN THE BAND (above)*

*SOME SINGLE REED INSTRUMENTS (top, right): clarinet, alto clarinet, bass clarinet*

*THE SAXOPHONE FAMILY (bottom, right): l. to r.: soprano, alto, tenor, baritone, bass*

*BRASSES IN THE BAND (above)*

*THE SOPRANO BRASSES (top, right): l. to r.: Flügel horn, cornet, trumpet*

*THE LOW BRASSES (bottom, right): front: baritones; middle: trombones; rear: sousaphones*

PSU
BLUE
BAND

PERCUSSIONS IN THE MARCHING BAND *(above): street drums, cymbals, bass drum*

SOME SMALL PERCUSSION INSTRUMENTS *(top, right): l. to r.: maracas, tambourine, claves, castanets, triangle*

OTHER PERCUSSION INSTRUMENTS *(bottom, right): l. to f.: timpani, bells, marimba, snare drum, bass drum, and cymbals; rear: chimes*

THE CONSOLE OF THE ELECTRIC ORGAN. *The drawbars appear above the upper keyboard.*

violins
clarinet (short passage)
oboe (short passage)
clarinet

*Tchaikovsky*

*Symphony No. 5*, second movement
strings (introduction)
horn
horn (clarinet countermelody)
oboe (horn countermelody)
clarinet–bassoon–basses (short passages)
'cellos (high register)
violins
clarinet
bassoon (high register)
'cellos–violins–'cellos–violins–woodwinds–violins–full orchestra
trumpets (trombones and timpani background)
pizzicato strings (introduction to original melody)
violins (low register, with oboe countermelody)
violins (with clarinet countermelody)
woodwinds (in octaves)
violins (with full orchestra)
trombones (with trumpet figures)
clarinet and bassoon (in octaves)
violins and lower strings
clarinet (at end of movement)

*Tchaikovsky*

*Symphony No. 5*, third movement
violins
oboe and bassoon (in octaves)
clarinet
clarinet and bassoon (in unison)
woodwinds
bassoon (in high register)

flute and clarinet (in octaves)
violins
violas
piccolo
high woodwinds and strings intermittent
violins
violas
oboe
violins
oboe and bassoon (in octaves)
clarinet
clarinet and bassoon (in unison)
woodwinds
bassoon (in high register)
flute and clarinet (in octaves)
violins
clarinet and bassoon (in unison)
violins
full orchestra

## *Stravinsky*

*Ronde des Princesses*, from *Firebird Suite*

(NOTE: This test record should not be used until after the others listed above have been studied, for in this recording some of the instruments have only one note, as for example the opening horn note; many have only four or five notes in the melody before the succeeding instrument takes over. The listing has been made horizontally, with each line representing a complete musical thought: if you get lost, try to pick up with the beginning of the next line.)

horn–flutes–solo violin
oboe–solo 'cello–clarinet–bassoon–horn–pizzicato bass
violins–'cellos–violins–horn–clarinet–horn–clarinet–flute–horn–flutes
oboe–solo 'cello–clarinet–bassoon–pizzicato bass

flute (low)—horn—flute—horn—violins—clarinet—violins—clarinet—flute—clarinet and horn—woodwinds—oboe and horn—violins—harp
oboe—clarinet—horn—clarinet—piccolo—oboe—horn—oboe—clarinet

## *Ravel*

*Bolero*
(NOTE: This is *not* a good record to use for learning instrumental timbre, for it is an example of the indefiniteness of instrumental sounds of the Impressionistic period, created by unusual instruments, the extreme ranges of more usual instruments, and unusual instrumental combinations. But it is interesting to follow: the instruments listed are those taking the melody, each line following the preceding one.)

flute
clarinet
bassoon
E-flat clarinet
oboe d'amour (an alto oboe in A)
flute and muted trumpet
tenor saxophone
sopranino saxophone in F
piccolos, horn, and celeste
oboes, clarinets, and English horn
trombone (high register)
flutes, piccolo, oboes, English horn, clarinets, and tenor saxophone
flutes, piccolo, clarinets, and violins
the above, plus English horn, tenor saxophone, and violins in four-part harmony
flutes, piccolo, oboes, English horn, trumpet, and unison violins
the above woodwinds, plus clarinets, soprano saxophone, trombone, violins, violas, and 'cellos

flutes, piccolo, oboes, saxophones, violins, and trumpets in four-part harmony
flutes, piccolo, clarinets, saxophones, violins, trombone, and trumpets in four-part harmony

## *The Instruments of the Band*

WHILE MANY INSTRUMENTS of the orchestra are also used in the band, some others are added to take care of the balance of tone and to substitute for the string choir, which is largely nonexistent in the band personnel. Originally an outdoor marching unit, the band made use of those instruments that could be played effectively under those circumstances. With the growth in popularity of the concert band, and its appearance under better conditions in concert halls or in specially built band-shells outdoors, the instrumentation has been changed. Many of our finest professional bands of the present day are primarily concert organizations, and many of our colleges and universities that have a need for both the marching and concert units change the instrumental balance in order to conform to the existing need.

### STRINGS IN THE BAND

Although there is no place for stringed instruments in the marching band, the *string bass* is being included in the instrumentation of the concert band. In ensemble work it plays music similar to that of the tubas but its most practical use and the reason for its inclusion is in carrying the bass notes when the tubas would be too heavy an underpinning for the softer treble instruments. There has also been an attempt to add a section of 'cellos to the concert band, but this does not seem to be gaining much favor. The only other stringed instrument included in the band make-up is the harp, which can be used effectively in the same way it is used with the orchestra.

### WOODWINDS IN THE BAND

The modern symphonic band, so called because its proportions compare with the instrumentation and size of the symphony orchestra, is so new in comparison with the traditional orchestra that there is not yet any established personnel. Band conductors disagree on proportions, and even publishers of band music have not standardized their products in terms of numbers of parts. Since the woodwinds of the band take the place of the strings of the orchestra to large degree, a great many are used; they are both more numerous and more diversified than in the symphony orchestra.

The woodwind choir in a good concert band would contain the following instruments, in proportions to suit the conductor. Those in parentheses do not always appear, largely because of their unavailability.

"No reeds"
- flutes
- piccolos

Single reeds
- E-flat clarinet
- B-flat clarinets
- alto clarinets
- bass clarinets
- (contrabass clarinets)
- alto saxophones
- tenor saxophones
- baritone saxophones
- (bass saxophone)

Double reeds
- oboes
- (English horn)
- bassoons
- (contrabassoon)

### THE "NO-REED" INSTRUMENTS

Band *flutes* are identical with orchestra flutes. Band *piccolos* differ only in the fact that they are slightly smaller and therefore slightly shriller in tone.

### THE SINGLE-REED INSTRUMENTS

Since the *B-flat clarinets* as used in the orchestra are considered in the band as substitutes for the violins, they are used in great numbers, from twenty-four to thirty-two being desirable depending upon the size of the band. Several *bass clarinets* are also used.

Additional members of the clarinet family in the band include the E-flat, the alto, and the contrabass. The *E-flat clarinet* is smaller and therefore higher than the *B-flat;* its music either doubles that of the solo clarinets or extends the clarinet range upward. The *alto clarinet* is midway in size between the two orchestra instruments; it resembles the bass clarinet in shape somewhat; its tone is pleasant though not very strong. The *contrabass clarinet* is built in two sizes which give it a range an octave lower than the alto clarinet or the bass clarinet. It is not written for by most band composers; when used it extends the clarinet timbre downward.

The *saxophone* family, well known from the use of its members in dance orchestras, is used to some degree in the band. Of the eight members of the family three and sometimes four different ones are included in the band. The *alto,* the *tenor,* and the *baritone saxophone* are the three sizes used in dance work as well as in the band; the *bass saxophone* sometimes makes its appearance, though rarely. It is interesting to note that saxophones were included as members of the symphony orchestra in the last century by some French composers, and have been scored for in the orchestra more recently by a few writers, but without gaining a foothold in that organization. But they have proven useful in the make-up of the band as harmony instruments covering a large part of the musical gamut. The saxophone is one of the easiest instruments to play, and one of the most difficult to play well.

#### THE DOUBLE-REED INSTRUMENTS

In all cases these are identical with the orchestra instruments.

### BRASSES IN THE BAND

The band utilizes more diversity in brasses as well as in woodwinds to give additional facility and additional tone color in the absence of the strings. These instruments can be listed in groups according to pitch ranges as follows:

cornet
trumpet
(Flügel horn)

French horn
(alto horn)
(mellophone)

trombone
baritone horn
euphonium

*E-flat* tuba
*BB-flat* tuba

#### THE HIGH BRASSES

In the band the *trumpet* takes second place in prominence to he *cornet*. This instrument is similar to the trumpet in method of performance and in range; it differs in having a larger bore, which gives a more mellow tone. Cornets are therefore used more constantly, and to advantage, while to the trumpets are left the passages in which more brilliant quality is desired. Separate parts are written for these two instruments of identical range, which shows how distinctly their difference in timbre is recognized. The third instrument of the group, identical in pitch with the other two, is the *Flügel horn,* which has a bore still larger than that of the cornet. It is not often found in the band ensemble, nor are special parts for it often contained in the band score.[11]

### THE MEDIUM-RANGE BRASSES

The *French horn* has come to be the instrument in its range preferred by band directors, but several substitute instruments are still used. Ease of playing may excuse the substitutions in the marching band, but there is no justification for not using the French horn in the concert band.

The two instruments in question are the alto horn and the mellophone. The *alto horn* is an upright instrument resembling the larger baritone horn or tuba, with the same fingering system that is used on the higher brasses; it sounds five notes deeper because of its size. The *mellophone* is basically the same as the alto horn, except that its shape has been changed so that it resembles to some extent the general curved outline of the French horn.

### THE LOWER-RANGE BRASSES

The *trombone* keeps its important place in this range group in the band, but other instruments of exactly the same range become important members of the ensemble. These are the *baritone horn* and the *euphonium*. These two instruments are similar in that they use the piston valve system of fingering; they differ in the size of the bore: the euphonium has the larger bore and therefore has a more mellow tone and its lower notes are better.

[11] According to the dictionary the correct pronunciation of *cornet* makes it rhyme with the word *hornet*. Common usage, however, permits the accent on the second syllable.

The same music is often used for the two instruments and either or both can perform in that section of the band. It was noted that the woodwinds of the band take the parts of most of the strings of the orchestra, but often the melodies that would be given to the 'cellos in the orchestra are taken by the baritone section of the band. Besides its pleasing tone the baritone or euphonium is better than the trombone in rapid passages because of the comparative simplicity in changing tones with the valves as versus the slide technique of the trombone.

### THE LOWEST BRASSES

The *tuba* continues, as in the orchestra, as the basic instrument of the brass choir, and while the performance techniques, ranges, and general timbre are the same, the instruments of the band look different, having undergone a metamorphosis for convenience in carrying. Three distinct forms of the instrument are used: the upright used in the orchestra and the *recording bass* (an upright with the bell opening facing front) are preferred for concert work. In the other form the tubing has been bent into such a shape that the weight of the instrument can be carried by the shoulder: this is more satisfactory for the marching band. This variation is known as the *sousaphone* in honor of John Philip Sousa, the American bandmaster and composer.

Both *E-flat* and *BB-flat* tubas were listed as band instruments. Actually these are only two of several key pitches in which the instruments are built, but they are the most popular ones. Because of the depth of all these instruments it is not necessary to try to differentiate between them either from the point of view of sound or appearance.

### PERCUSSIONS IN THE BAND

Because of the original function of the band its percussion instruments take on a far more important role than they do in the orchestra. The snare drums have greater depth for ease in carrying on the march and for the additional volume, but otherwise the same instruments, either identical or nearly so, are used and perform the same general services that were stated in the discussion on the percussion instruments of the orchestra.

## *The Keyboard Instruments*

Two well-known instruments that are independent units within themselves are the piano and the organ. This independence rests on the fact that each instrument cannot only play a melody, but can accompany itself. With the exception of the harp and several of the percussion instruments of definite pitch, all of the orchestra and band instruments discussed are limited by their construction to playing one single tone at a time. It is necessary to combine several or many of these instruments into quartets or orchestras or bands to produce instrumental harmony.

But harmony is the natural accomplishment of the piano and organ, since ten or more notes can be sounded simultaneously by the use of the fingers, and, in the case of the organ, the feet. From the harmonic point of view one instrument can do what it takes ten or more other instruments to do in combination.

Since harmony is one of the five fundamentals of music, its importance is recognized even in the performance of solo instruments. It would be very monotonous to hear even the greatest violinist give a complete concert without benefit of piano accompaniment. The inclusion of the piano does not detract from the genius of the violinist but rather adds to the interest of the music he is performing by furnishing the background that will point up his playing to the listener. And a fine singer performing in a church needs the complement of the organ background to give the most meaning to his singing.

THE PIANO

The *piano* was invented to fill the need for an instrument that could not only play harmonically, but that would be capable of producing changes in volume of tone that were impossible on its predecessors except in a very mechanical and unsatisfactory way. The two chief piano predecessors were the *harpsichord* and the *clavichord* (and their variants) which had served for many years both as solo instruments and accompanying instruments, and in combination with melody instruments. They were useful but the limitation noted kept them from being completely satisfactory.

The two differed in their mechanism, although both, like the piano, were actuated by a combination of the principles involved in the percussion and stringed instruments: a key was struck which caused a string to respond. The clavichord mechanism caused a metal tangent to touch the string; in the harpsichord the string was plucked by a quill.

The piano utilizes an action whereby the force exerted on the keyboard is transferred to the string in terms of volume. The action also gives immediate release of the hammer as soon as it has struck the string, which permits free vibration until the depressed key has been released. The manual action can be further improved by either muting or sustaining the vibration of the strings by the use of the several pedals. From the early eighteenth century when the instrument was invented and called a *piano e forte* (later *pianoforte*) or "soft and loud" to emphasize its qualifications, there have been numerous changes in the action, the shape, and the size of the instruments.[12]

[12] Many of these changes were the result of work done by American manufacturers. One of the most obvious changes of recent years has been the size of the instrument: the practical problem of owning a piano that could be placed in a small room without overbalancing the other furnishings has been solved by the manufacture of the spinet model piano, which, incidentally, takes its name from a square-shaped harpsichord of the Renaissance period.

### THE ORGAN

The history of the *organ* goes back several thousand years to the early Greek and Hebrew civilizations. Almost every country has had some variation of this instrument in its musical development, and while there are tremendous differences in the instruments they all have had this common factor: the sound is produced by forcing air through pipes by means other than lung power. The air reservoir and its method of control, the types and sizes of the pipes, the multiplicity of keyboards in the console, the mechanics for simplifying performance, and other features have all undergone experimentation and refinement through the centuries.

Some musicologists believe that the organ reached its highest point of perfection in the eighteenth and nineteenth centuries and that the many additions that have been made since that time add more to its size and complexity than to its musicalness. If the organ is to be considered an instrument that attempts to sound like a combination of orchestra and band with percussive effects as well as those of all varieties of woodwind, brass, and string timbres, then some of the twentieth-century instruments would have to be considered the last word in organ construction. But if the organ is considered from the point of view of what it was meant to be, namely a unit with its own basic timbre plus variations that would add qualities for contrast in the various manuals, the modern titans have gone far beyond the goal. Unfortunately, it seems that in the eyes of the general public bigness has been substituted for musical quality as a basis for judgment.

Organs are built with from two to seven manuals, or keyboards for the hands, plus a complete pedal keyboard for the feet. Each keyboard controls a number of series of speaking pipes depending on the size of the instrument. In addition there are couplers which will give to one single key the ability to play that pitch in any or all of the tone colors controlled by that particular manual, or to sound tones normally controlled by one of the other manuals, or to sound not only these tones but similar tones an octave lower or an octave or some other interval higher, or, with the aid of the so-called mixtures, to sound many pitches simultaneously. The feet also control by pedal action the apparatus which opens and closes the vents leading into the chambers where the pipes are housed, to give shading in volume to a sound coming from a particular group of pipes. All in all it is a very complicated affair.

Although the basic mechanics of playing existing organs are rather well standardized, instruments built by different companies and even different instruments built by the same company are so dissimilar that an organist needs time to get acquainted with a strange instrument before publicly performing on it. Incidentally, the architecturally beautiful pipes that are seen over the organ loft in churches are generally nonspeaking pipes, and are placed there for eye appeal only.

The comparatively recent *electric organ* is built on a principle completely different from that of the pipe organ. Instead of pipes of various materials and shapes to imitate various timbres, the electric organ utilizes the variables of the overtone series present. A series of drawbars can be set, each in any of eight positions to conform to the acoustical ratio of the tonal harmonics as analyzed by the oscillograph. This gives a fairly accurate reproduction of various instrumental timbres.

The electric organ has a place in our musical life, chiefly because of its movability and its relative inexpensiveness. It should be thought of, however, as a separate instrument in its own right and not as a substitute for the pipe organ.

## *SUGGESTED LISTENING*

### *Harpsichord*

Bach: *Goldberg Variations*
Bach: *Well-Tempered Clavier*
Bach: English Suites
Bach: French Suites
Handel: Suites
Scarlatti, D.: Sonatas

### *Clavichord*

Bach: Two Part Inventions

### *Piano*

Piano concertos or independent compositions by such composers as Chopin, Schumann, Liszt, Brahms, Beethoven, Mozart, Bartók, Gershwin, Debussy, Ravel, de Falla, Mendelssohn, Grieg, and others

### *Organ*

Bach: Chorale Preludes
Bach: *Toccata and Fugue in D minor*
Bach: *St. Anne Prelude and Fugue*
Bach: *Passacaglia and Fugue in C minor*
Bach: *Fantasia and Fugue in G minor*
Buxtehude: Organ music
Franck: *Grand Pièce Symphonique*
Handel: Concerti for organ
Sowerby: *Symphony for Organ in G*
Widor: *Variations from Symphonie Gothique*

CHAPTER 3

# *Rhythm*

IN DEALING with the five fundamentals of music appreciation the subject of timbre has been discussed first because it seemed logical to start with the human voice which is a part of all of us, and to follow this up with the instrumental voices that go to make up another segment of our music. If the procedure had been chronological, rhythm would have been studied first, because musicologists agree that the first type of music was rhythmic. This seems logical, since music was originally a useful art rather than a fine art, and took its place in the life of the tribe: rhythmic music no doubt served early man as an accompaniment to the action of his dances, which were part of his religion as well as his entertainment.

A dictionary definition of *rhythm* mentions "movement characterized by regular, measured, or harmonious recurrence of stress, beat, sound, accent or motion." This defines rhythm in its larger sense, and will serve as a background for the musical application of the rhythmic principle. In the larger sense there is rhythm in the natural phenomena: day and night, the passing of the seasons, the flow of the tides. There is rhythm in physiology: the beat of the pulse, regular breathing. There is rhythm in athletics: the strokes of a fine crew in a racing shell, or the strides of a hurdler or distance runner.

Rhythm in music suggests the same sort of flow of motion with recurring high points of emphasis and intervening relaxation. For a working definition we suggest, musically speaking, that rhythm is the regular recurrence of accented and unaccented beats.

Examine that definition. The regular recurrence of the accents is important, but it is the unaccented beats that give character to the rhythm and make the differentiation between various types of rhythms. A series of accents, with no intervening lack of stresses would present merely a monotonous pounding and would fail to have any rhythmic significance.

In order to understand this fundamental of our music it is necessary to delve into certain theoretical phases of the music, but this can be done very nicely without getting into too technical a discussion. First, however, you should be cautioned against using the word *time* in relation to music. Admittedly this is often done, as the following four statements will show. Each of these statements can be understood, but each would be more definitive if a different word were used in place of *time*. Recognizing these differences and using the proper musical vocabulary will save confusion later on.

1. "This music is in a very fast *time*." That you understand.
2. "This music is in three-four *time*." That you will also understand if you have had even the beginning of a musical education.
3. "This music is in syncopated *time*." This should also mean something to you.
4. "This music takes four minutes' *time* to play." In this statement, when *time* refers to actual duration, the word may be used without fear of confusion, but even here *duration* would do just as well or better.

Sentences 1, 2, and 3 may be understood, partially because of their proximity, but it is obvious that the word *time* is being overworked, for three completely different meanings have been assigned to it. For clarity it would be better to say:

1. "This music is in a very fast *tempo.*" *Tempo* signifies the speed of a composition.

2. "This music is in three-four *meter.*" *Meter* refers to the measure sign at the beginning of the composition and the resultant quantitative make-up of each measure of the composition.

3. "This music is in a syncopated *rhythm.*" As suggested in an earlier paragraph *rhythm* has to do with the recurrence of the pulsations.

Since rhythm actually depends upon a combination of tempo and meter, it would be helpful to look into these two interdependent subjects to get to the background of the rhythm itself. For example, when we speak of a waltz rhythm, we know that the music has a certain number of beats to the measure, and that it is to be played at a certain speed. If the meter is changed, it can no longer be waltz rhythm, and if the music is performed too rapidly or too slowly the characteristics of the waltz rhythm are also lost.

## *TEMPO*

The *tempo* of any musical composition may be set exactly by the composer, or he may suggest in a general way an approximate speed so that the performer will have some leeway in his interpretation. In some cases, particularly in very early compositions, we find that there is no hint of the speed given: in these cases the interpreter must either go by tradition or must use his best musical judgment to get the best musical effect.

To show the exact speed he wants for the performance of his composition the composer may use a symbol at the beginning of his music, placed above the first staff. For example, — MM ♩= 120. The MM (sometimes this is omitted and just the note value and rate are given) refers to Maelzel's Metronome, a mechanical device consisting of a spring and a sliding weight on a graduated scale pendulum. When the weight is set at 120 and the lever released, it will give audible ticks at the rate of 120 per minute. More recently an electrically operated metronome which gives the same results has come on the market. If the performer does not happen to have either of these instruments, he can figure out the tempo suggested by trial and error with the use of a stop watch or any timepiece that has a second hand. When the 120 pulsations per minute have been established, the performer assigns each tick to a note of the valuation given in the original symbol.

A second method used to designate tempo, and one that gives some leeway to the performer, is the use of tempo terms. These generally appear in the Italian language, which has become the adopted language of theoretical musicians, although some composers have used similar words in their own language to give more exact directions. (The Italian terms are general because music writing was developed in Italy in connection with the music of the Early Christian Church. While the texts were in Latin, directions for performance were in the common language of the Italian fathers; as the hand-copied manuscripts of these worthy fathers spread to churches in other countries, the original directive language was retained.)

These Italian tempo terms are purely relative and any one of them might have a slightly different meaning to different interpreters: in fact, even the best conductors will sometimes direct the same composition at slightly different speeds at various performances, though they might feel that they were doing it exactly the same way each time. There are a large number of these terms, just as there are a number of ways to express speed in the English language. It is not necessary to know all of them unless you plan to interpret music either as a soloist or as a conductor. However, seven of the most common ones are listed to give you an idea of the relative use of some of the more important words.

This basic vocabulary is very helpful to know, and to those of you who wish to read scores as you follow the recordings they will give an insight into what is expected, for they will appear a great many times. A musical dictionary will take care of those words not listed here. The following are in order from the slowest to the fastest.

*largo:* very, very slow; literally "broad"
*adagio:* very slow, but faster than *largo*; think of this in connection with the slow-moving *adagio* dancers
*andante:* slow
*moderato:* moderate tempo; neither slow nor fast
*allegro:* fast; literally "happy," with the idea that if you do something in a happy way you will act a bit faster than you might otherwise
*vivace:* very fast; "vivacious" children will act faster than "happy" adults
*presto:* very, very fast; the magician says "*presto chango*"—"the hand is quicker than the eye"; a *presto* is a speed as fast as the musicians can perform the notes involved.

## *SUGGESTED LISTENING*

### *Tempo Terms*

#### *Largo*

Berlioz: *Symphonie Fantastique*, introduction to first movement
Dvořák: *From the New World Symphony*, second movement
Grofé: *Cloudburst*, from *Grand Canyon Suite*, beginning
Handel: *Ombra mai fu*, from *Xerxes*
Mussorgsky: *Catacombs*, from *Pictures at an Exhibition*
Tchaikovsky: *1812 Overture*, beginning
Prokofiev: *Classical Symphony*, second movement (*larghetto:* not quite as slow as *largo*)
Rimsky-Korsakov: *Scheherazade Suite*, beginning of first movement (*largo e maestoso:* very, very slow and majestic)

## *Adagio*

Berlioz: *Symphonie Fantastique*, third movement
Brahms: *Symphony No. 1*, introduction to first movement
Dvořák: *From the New World Symphony*, introduction to first movement
Haydn: *Clock Symphony*, introduction to first movement
Haydn: *Surprise Symphony*, introduction to first movement
Mozart: *Symphony No. 39 in E-flat major*, introduction to first movement
Weber: *Overture* to *Der Freischütz*, beginning
Brahms: *Symphony No. 2*, second movement (*adagio non troppo:* very slow, but not too much so)
Beethoven: *Eroica Symphony*, second movement (*adagio assai:* very slow)
Tchaikovsky: *Symphonie Pathétique*, introduction to first movement; and fourth movement (*adagio lamentoso:* slow and with sadness)

## *Andante*

Berlioz: *Roman Carnival Overture*, after introduction
Brahms: *Symphony No. 3*, second movement
Haydn: *Clock Symphony*, second movement
Haydn: *Surprise Symphony*, second movement
Listz: *Les Préludes*, beginning
Mozart: *Eine Kleine Nachtmusik*, second movement
Mozart: *Symphony No. 40 in G minor*, second movement
Mussorgsky: *Old Castle*, from *Pictures at an Exhibition*
Saint-Saëns: from the *Carnival of the Animals: Tortoise,* and *Cuckoo in the Woods*
Tchaikovsky: *Symphony No. 5*, introduction to first movement
Beethoven: *Symphony No. 5*, second movement (*andante con moto:* slow, with motion)
Brahms: *Symphony No. 4*, second movement (*andante moderato:* moderately slow)
Mendelssohn: *Nocturne*, from *Midsummer Night's Dream* (*andante tranquillo:* slow and tranquil)

Mozart: *Symphony No. 41*, second movement (*andante cantabile:* slow and in a singing style)
Tchaikovsky: *Symphony No. 4*, introduction to first movement (*andante sostenuto:* slow and sustained)
Tchaikovsky: *Dance of the Sugar Plum Fairy*, from the *Nutcracker Suite* (*andante non troppo:* slow, but not too slow)
Wagner: *Overture* to *Tannhäuser* (*andante maestoso:* slow and majestic)

## *Moderato*

Debussy: *Nuages*, from *Nocturnes*
Ravel: *Bolero*
Saint-Saëns: *Danse Macabre*
Tchaikovsky: *Dance of the Toy Flutes*, from the *Nutcracker Suite*

## *Allegro*

Beethoven: *Symphony No. 5*, third and fourth movements
Berlioz: *Symphonie Fantastique*, fifth movement
Brahms: *Symphony No. 3*, fourth movement
Brahms: *Academic Festival Overture*, beginning
Gershwin: *Piano Concerto*, first movement
Mozart: *Concerto for Horn in E-flat major*, first movement
Mozart: *Eine Kleine Nachtmusik*, first and fourth movements
Prokofiev: *Classical Symphony*, first movement
Tchaikovsky: *Symphony No. 4*, third movement
Beethoven: *Eroica Symphony*, fourth movement (*allegro molto:* much speed)
Beethoven: *Symphony No. 5*, first movement (*allegro con brio:* fast, with brilliance)
Brahms: *Symphony No. 2*, first movement (*allegro non troppo:* fast, but not too fast)
Brahms: *Symphony No. 2*, fourth movement (*allegro con spirito:* fast, with spirit)
Brahms: *Symphony No. 4*, third movement (*allegro giocoso:* fast and joyous)
Dvořák: *From the New World Symphony*, fourth movement (*allegro con fuoco:* fast, with fire)

Franck: *Symphony in D minor*, second movement (*allegretto:* a little slower than *allegro*)
Tchaikovsky: *Symphony No. 6*, second movement (*allegro con grazia:* fast, with grace)

### *Vivace*

Dukas: *Sorcerer's Apprentice*, after introduction
Haydn: *Clock Symphony*, fourth movement
Rimsky-Korsakov: *Flight of the Bumble Bee*, from *Tsar Sultan*
Wagner: *Ride of the Valkyries*, from *Die Walküre*
Beethoven: *Symphony No. 9*, second movement (*molto vivace:* a bit faster than *vivace*)
Dvořák: *From the New World Symphony*, third movement (*molto vivace*)
Mendelssohn: *Scherzo*, from *Midsummer Night's Dream* (*allegro vivace:* somewhere between *allegro* and *vivace*)
Prokofiev: *Classical Symphony*, fourth movement (*molto vivace*)
Tchaikovsky: *Russian Dance*, from the *Nutcracker Suite* (*molto vivace*)

### *Presto*

Beethoven: *Symphony No. 7*, third movement
Beethoven: *Symphony No. 9*, beginning of fourth movement
Glinka: *Russlan and Ludmila Overture*
Haydn: *Clock Symphony*, first movement, after introduction
Saint-Saëns: *Wild Horses*, from the *Carnival of the Animals* (*presto furioso:* fast and furious)

## *METER*

Certain phases of music are closely allied to mathematics. One of these phases is *meter*, which is shown by the fractionlike numbers at the beginning of a musical composition. In this meter signature the upper numeral refers to the number of beats in a measure; the lower refers to the type of note that will receive the beat. (The measure referred to is an arbitrary unit of musical measurement; each measure is separated from those adjacent by the vertical lines or bars drawn through the musical staff.) In each measure of a composition the total value of the notes must add up to correspond with the meter signature. This is a matter of simple fractions. For instance, in ¾ meter, the measure might include 3 quarter notes, or 6 eighth notes, or 2 quarter notes and 4 sixteenth notes, or any other combination that would add up correctly. (Since pauses in music are quite important, rests of equal value can be considered in place of all or some of the notes in any given measure.)

The number of beats in the measure, designated by the upper half of the meter sign, may be almost any number in the low range. The most commonly used are 2, 3, 4, and 6; less common, but sometimes found, are 9, 12, 5, 7, and 1. The type of note that will get the beat, as designated by the lower half of the meter sign, will be the quarter, the eighth, the sixteenth or the half, represented by the numerals 4, 8, 16, or 2.

The best way to study meter is by getting an actual physical reaction or feel to what is designated by the meter sign. This can be done by going through the basic motions used by a conductor as he leads a group. For this purpose imagine that the music is in a *moderato* or *andante* tempo, for as it gets slower or faster complications set in.

Since the first beat of any measure is the accented pulsation, the conductor will use a downbeat to represent it, for this stroke is stronger than one to the side or straight up.[1] No matter what the meter, the first beat will always be down as shown on a diagram of the tip of a conductor's baton by a vertical line and an arrow representing direction:

[1] If you don't believe this, try to drive a spike into a board using a sidestroke or an upstroke; then try it with a downstroke.

Now comes the importance of the unaccented beats, for the pattern will depend on how many of these secondary beats must be included before we are ready to start the next identical measure. But no matter how many there are, as a matter of expediency the final beat must be made with an upsweep so that we are ready to start the next measure from the original position:

In the case of two-beat music (whether it is 2/2 or 2/4 or 2/8) the beat would look like this:

Force is used on the important first downbeat, which bounces back from the bottom of the stroke; the unaccented second beat is not as energetic and is picked up as the hand reverts to its starting position. As you try this pattern think the emphasis: *BOOM ta BOOM ta BOOM ta BOOM ta,* until you get the feel of it, and as the pattern becomes more automatic whistle your favorite march with it and you will see that it fits.

For three-beat music, beat #1 is the same; beat #2 goes out to the right; beat #3 returns to the starting position: *BOOM ta ta BOOM ta ta BOOM ta ta;* and then hum along with the *Missouri Waltz* or some other waltz tune.

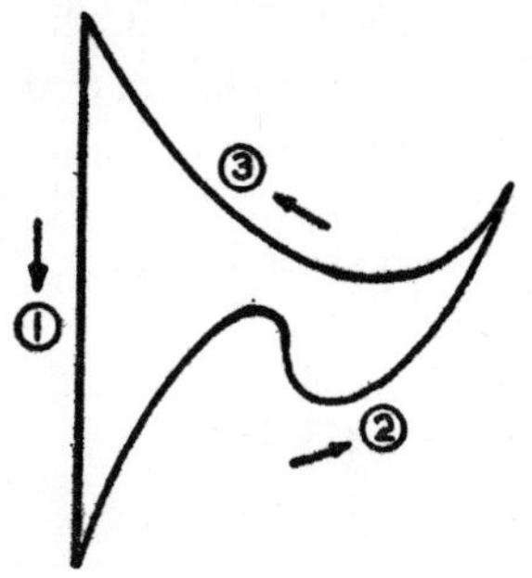


In four-beat music we find that no matter how hard we try we can't have the three unaccented beats of exactly the same value: #3 will feel as if it needs a little more stress or attention than will #2 and #4. So we start off again with the usual downbeat on #1; take a short stroke across the body to the left for #2; a larger swoop out to the far right will give the minor accent #3 seems to need; back up to the starting point for #4.

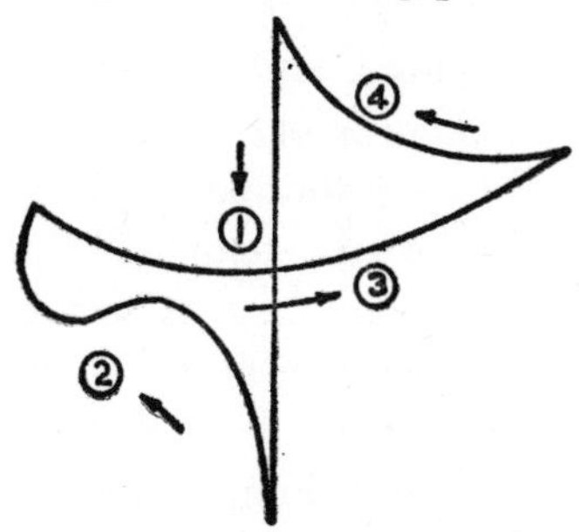

*BOOM ta* TA *ta BOOM ta* TA *ta,* with the second TA a bit more pronounced than the other two. Try *Onward, Christian Soldiers* or *Old Man River* for this one.

The six-beat measure is likewise composed of both a major and a minor accent: *BOOM ta ta* TA *ta ta,* or *ONE two three* FOUR *five six.* (All meters except the two-beat and three-beat are considered compound meters, with one or more secondary accents in addition to the first-beat accent.) In six-beat music the hand comes down, bounces slightly to the left, then farther to the left; #4 is across the body to the right, #5 makes an arc toward the starting position and #6 returns to the start. After the pattern is set in your mind and in your muscular reaction start *Drink to Me Only with Thine Eyes* on the downbeat.

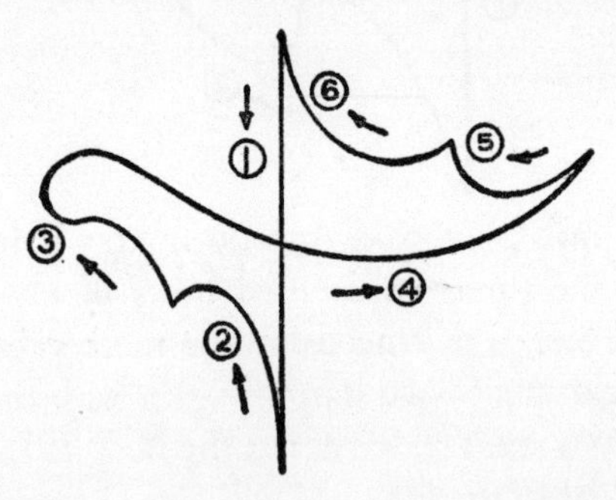


If you have done this pattern-beating conscientiously, you should feel the intimate relationship between the path of the arm and the accents of the music. After you think you have these beats well established, there is one good way to prove this relationship: get a good strong four-beat routine going and have someone play a waltz in the same tempo. If this doesn't seem incorrect and confusing to you, there is something wrong with your rhythmic sense. In fact, you probably shuffle along in the same plodding way on a dance floor whether the orchestra is playing a waltz, a slow blues, a jump tune, or whatever.

## *Meters*

(At a tempo slow enough so that the music can be followed with the conducting pattern given in the text)

### *2-beat*

Tchaikovsky: from the *Nutcracker Suite: Overture Miniature; Dance of the Sugar Plum Fairy; Russian Dance; Dance of the Toy Flutes*
Haydn: *Surprise Symphony*, second and fourth movements
Beethoven: *Symphony No. 3*, fourth movement
Beethoven: *Symphony No. 7*, second movement
Brahms: *Symphony No. 1*, third movement
Dvořák: *From the New World Symphony*, first movement, after introduction
Mozart: *Symphony No. 39*, second movement

### *3-beat*

Grieg: *Anitra's Dance*, from *Peer Gynt Suite*
Ravel: *Bolero*
Tchaikovsky: from the *Nutcracker Suite: Arabian Dance; Waltz of the Flowers*
Berlioz: *Roman Carnival Overture*, after the introduction
Beethoven: *Symphony No. 5*, second movement
Brahms: *Symphony No. 1*, second movement
Brahms: *Symphony No. 2*, first movement
Franck: *Symphony in D minor*, second movement
Schubert: *Unfinished Symphony*, first and second movements
Tchaikovsky: *Symphony No. 5*, third movement
Tchaikovsky: *Symphony No. 6*, fourth movement
Sibelius: *Valse Triste*

### *4-beat*

Grieg: *Ase's Death* from *Peer Gynt Suite*
Tchaikovsky: from the *Nutcracker Suite: Marche; Chinese Dance*

Prokofiev: *Classical Symphony*, third movement (starts on third beat)
Beethoven: *Symphony No. 5*, fourth movement
Brahms: *Symphony No. 1*, fourth movement, after introduction
Brahms: *Symphony No. 3*, second movement
Dvořák: *From the New World Symphony*, fourth movement
Tchaikovsky: *Symphony No. 6*, third movement, second theme
Saint-Saëns: *Introduction and March of the Lions*, from the *Carnival of the Animals*

*6-beat*

Grieg: *Morning Mood*, from *Peer Gynt Suite*
Saint-Saëns: *The Swan*, from the *Carnival of the Animals*
Rimsky-Korsakov: *Scheherazade Suite*, third movement
Brahms: *Symphony No. 4*, second movement
Mozart: *Symphony No. 40*, second movement

*5-beat*

Tchaikovsky: *Symphony No. 6*, second movement
Rimsky-Korsakov: *Russian Easter Overture*, beginning

*9-beat and 12-beat music* is usually conducted as 3-beat and 4-beat music, respectively, using the major and minor accents only, and omitting the unaccented notes.

## *RHYTHM*

The *meter* and the *tempo* combine to give a feeling of pulsation that we call the *rhythm* of the composition. This rhythm may easily fall into a category of march, or waltz, or jig, or some other specified type, or it may merely have a feeling of a flow with accents here and there that is impossible to describe by any such simple term. But if the feeling is there, the rhythm is present.

The term *syncopation* needs explaining, for it seems contradictory to the explanation of rhythm that has been suggested. Syncopation is a type of rhythm, but it is the exception to the rule, for in syncopation accents are put into the music where they would not normally fall according to the rhythmic pattern involved. They are forced accents, not natural, and stop the normal flow of the true rhythm. Yet underlying these unnaturally placed accents the natural pulsation is either consciously or unconsciously maintained in our minds. This point can be proved in dancing, for the modern dance orchestra uses much syncopation in its performance and yet we continue to dance to the basic beat no matter how far afield the syncopation may go. If the basic beat was not felt, one good syncopated figure in the orchestra would cause every couple on the dance floor to stop or trip or get completely out of step, which obviously is not the case!

# *Melody*

OF THE five fundamentals of music, *melody* is the most obvious to the listener, for it is through melody in large part that we claim familiarity with music. One of our most able radio and television musicians says, "The tune's the thing," and for most of us he is right. The tune *is* the thing: it is the thing that we hear with the least amount of effort and it is the thing in music that we can best recall by whistling or humming later on. It is interesting to note that while this same entertainer realizes that "the tune's the thing" that first attracts us, he is smart enough to dress up the tune with interesting harmonies and attractive rhythms, and to give his presentation the variety of timbre possible with the use of his orchestra and vocal groups.

Melody, or tune, is both so obvious and so complex that it is hard to define. Sir Hubert Parry takes five columns in *Grove's Dictionary of Music and Musicians* for a definition, and after branching off into a discussion of both rhythm and harmony practically admits defeat. A more concise definition is this: melody consists of a succession of notes having a definite relationship to one another and to a key tone. "A succession of notes" without a modifying clause is not enough, for if we turn our backs to the piano keyboard and strike a lot of notes willy-nilly the result is not necessarily a melody. The modifying clause used above is a safeguard against this hodge-podge possibility.

In spite of the fact that the dictionary definition calls melody "an agreeable succession of sounds" our working definition is careful to make no reference to the idea that a melody line must have a pleasing or agreeable effect, for immediately upon assuming that such is true we get into the matter of subjective opinion, and would have to be able to answer the question "pleasing to whom?" in a satisfactory way, which is impossible. In fact, composers have on occasion deliberately written passages with a melody meant to be unpleasant in order to get certain emotional reactions.

The complications involved in a study of melody should be obvious. It is so closely allied to the other fundamentals of music that it is impossible to segregate it completely. An examination of its dependence to each of the other four fundamentals should prove this.

*Melody and timbre.* A single tone blown on a trumpet will give you the distinguishing timbre of that instrument, so it is possible to have timbre without melody. But if a melody is produced by any means whatsoever, either vocal or instrumental, it is necessary to have present the timbre of the producing agent.

*Melody and rhythm.* Various rhythms may be produced on the snare drum without benefit of melody. But when a melody is sounded, there must be notes of various lengths falling into a pattern, and the natural accents will appear; thus melody also includes rhythm as one of its parts.

*Melody and harmony.* Here the relationship is not as obvious, and it is quite true that a melody can be played or sung without benefit of a harmonic background. It is also true that, while harmony was brought into being to enhance melodies, the melody itself, in spite of many passing tones, will be based on the notes of the harmonic structure underlying it.

*Melody and form.* Form in music is its structure and is based on repetition of melody. Every tune, no matter how simple, has a distinct form.

Therefore, when you make the statement that such-and-such is your favorite tune, it would be well to examine the thing objectively to make sure that your statement is correct. Do you actually like a particular composition because of the melody alone? Or is it the underlying rhythm that appeals to you, or the harmonic pattern, or the repetition in form, or perhaps the quality of the performance? Or could it be the circumstances under which you first heard the music, or the person you were with at the time?

In judging good melody there are two things to keep in mind: (1) Don't use your ability to reproduce a tune by whistling or singing as a criterion of its worth, for many of the finest instrumental melodies are actually far out of the range of human vocal reproduction. (2) If a melody is new, such as in the great outpouring of popular music, your judgment is as good as that of anyone else. But if the music has lasted over the years with uncounted repetitions heard by numerous persons, it is wise to let their opinions influence yours to the extent of many repetitive listenings on your part until the beauty of the melody makes itself felt, if such is necessary.

CHAPTER 7

# Harmony

FORMAL courses in harmony and its related fields occupy a considerable amount of the time spent in training the professional musician. From the relative simplicity of combining two notes as an interval to the complexities of counterpoint and fugue, these courses may follow one after another for three or four years in the academic and artistic training of the theoretical musician. In our general course which has as its goal the application of facts about many phases of music to the listening program, it is obviously impossible to deal in more than harmonic generalities. It must be left to the harmony courses as such to give us the scientific "why" behind these larger aspects.

The word *harmony* has a larger connotation than its application to music. It is an "accord in feeling, manner, or action; as the *harmony* of a loving family; *harmony* of different causes." In art it is "a normal state of completeness in the relations of things to each other." In its relation to music, *harmony* may be defined as the simultaneous sounding of two or more tones, bearing a definite relationship to each other. This definition might not satisfy the harmony technicians, but it can be used as a working basis for this discussion; its terms are intentionally simplified to parallel the definition used for melody in the preceding section.

In the discussion of melody the purpose of harmony was suggested as being an effort to increase the enjoyment of a melody line by enriching it with a background of other tones. While this is not the sole aim of harmonic study, it is one of its major aspects and the one that is most applicable to listening to music. Several homely situations will help to explain this point.

You might enjoy hearing a good voice singing the tune of *Let Me Call You Sweetheart* in a locker room after a golf game, but the addition of three other voices to his melody should add to your enjoyment if, of course, the other three members of the impromptu quartet are capable of good harmonizing. You might marvel at the tone and technique of a great violinist in recital, but you would probably sneak out before the end if he showed up without an accompanist to add piano harmony to his violin playing. If you have not studied piano, you probably get satisfaction from being able to pick out a tune with one finger on the keyboard; if you progress by your own endeavors to the place where you can add other notes with the left hand to the right-hand melody, your satisfaction is increased many times. Except for some of our great religious music of the Jewish Synagogue and Roman Catholic Church in particular, all of our finest music is harmonized music. Whether or not we understand the rules behind the writing of harmony, we know that its presence is important in the total effect.

There is one phase of harmony that can be understood without too much technical background that will aid us as we listen to music. This is the difference between major and minor harmony and how these two are used in musical composition. To get to the sources of these harmonies it is necessary to go back to the various types of scale patterns in which our music is written. These fall into three main categories: chromatic, whole-tone, and diatonic. (Exceptions need not be considered here.) In considering scale patterns it must be understood that the smallest tonal musical measurement is called the half step. (Again there are unimportant exceptions.) The half step is represented on the piano keyboard as the tonal distance between any key and the next one to it, using the back part of the keyboard so that the black keys will not be overlooked. (The piano keyboard will be used for charting patterns and chords throughout this discussion as the most practical and obvious approach.)

The chromatic scale pattern would be represented by the intervals 1/2, 1/2, 1/2, 1/2, etc., since it is a series of half steps. The scale can be heard by playing the notes on the piano in order, not skipping any white or black keys as you progress upward or downward.

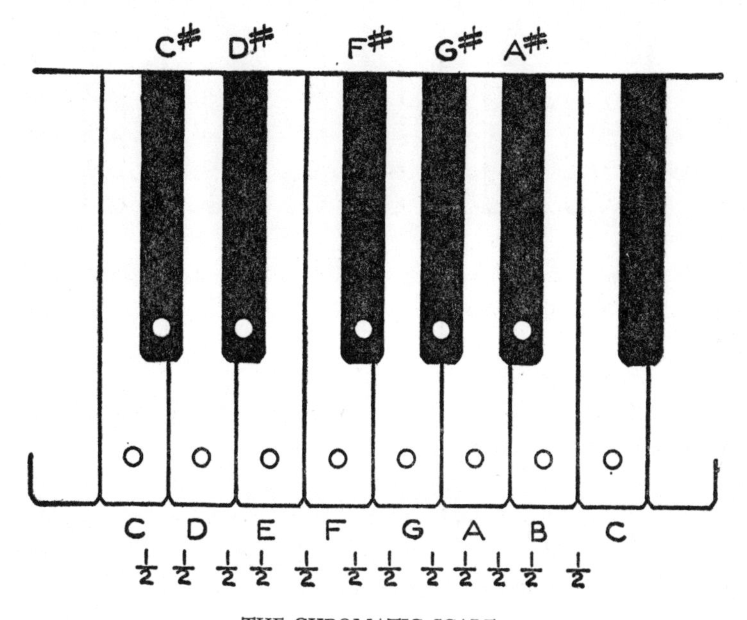


THE CHROMATIC SCALE

Piano keys to be played in this scale and those following are marked with a small circle.

The pattern for the whole-tone scale is represented by 1, 1, 1, 1, 1, 1. Each note is a whole step from the preceding (a whole step being the sum of two half steps.) A whole-tone scale as it is played on a piano keyboard has been sketched for your use. Play it and you will see that it does not sound very much like the *do-re-mi's* you might have learned in school. But it does have a use in a specialized type of music that will be discussed later in this book.

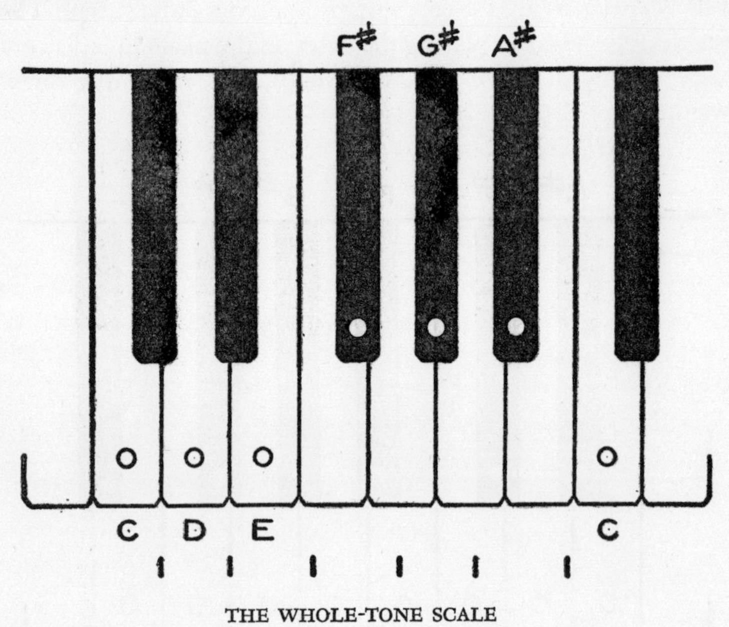


THE WHOLE-TONE SCALE

The diatonic scale is the one that is the basis for most of the music that we hear. The term diatonic suggests that in the pattern both whole steps and half steps are used in various but definite systems. These systems are known as the major diatonic and minor diatonic scales. The major scale pattern, 1, 1, 1/2, 1, 1, 1, 1/2, is always in that order. If you play the several major scales charted, you will find that you get the same relative tonal results no matter where you start. By studying these examples you should also understand why key signatures are used at the beginning of musical compositions. To prevent monotony, and because certain tonalities fit certain instruments and voices better than others, all music does not start on the same pitch, nor is it within the same confines. The scales used, therefore, may start on any pitch on the piano. But in all of these keys except one the pattern calls for the use of black notes to a smaller or larger de-

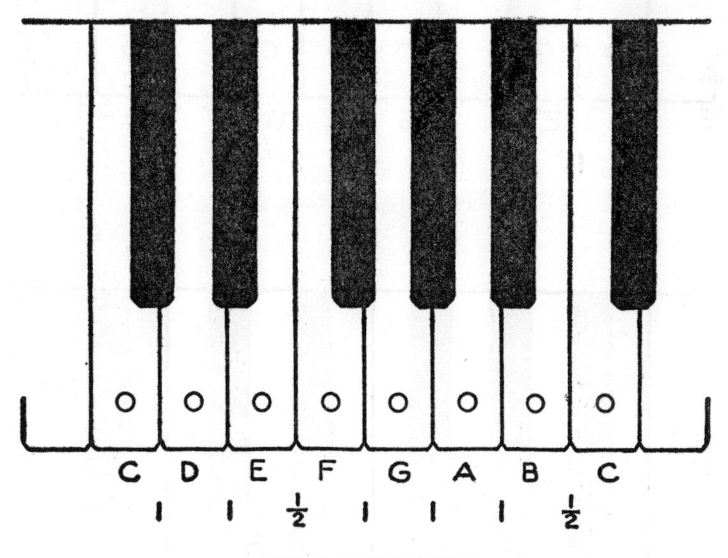


THE C-MAJOR SCALE

gree. Since these notes will be used throughout the entire composition, it is expedient to let one symbol (sharp or flat) for each such note be placed at the beginning of the composition, rather than having a symbol used every time the note appears in the composition itself. It is understood that this pilot sharp or flat will modify all the notes by that letter name throughout the work.

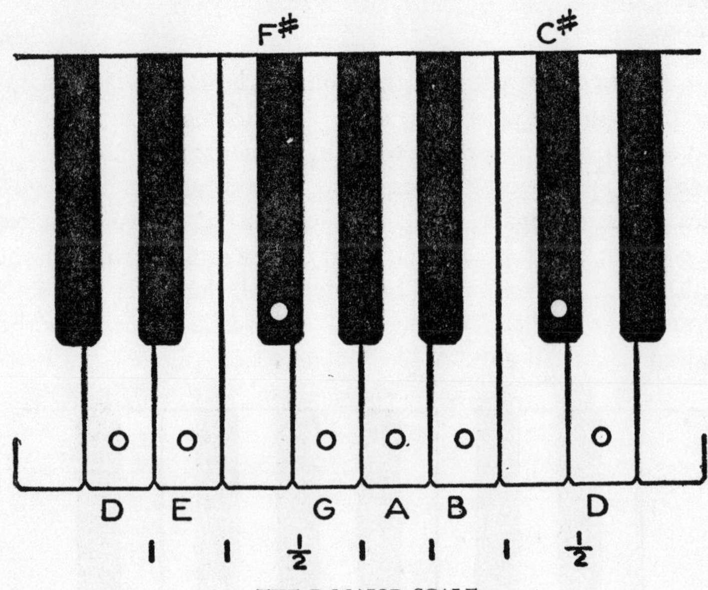

THE D-MAJOR SCALE

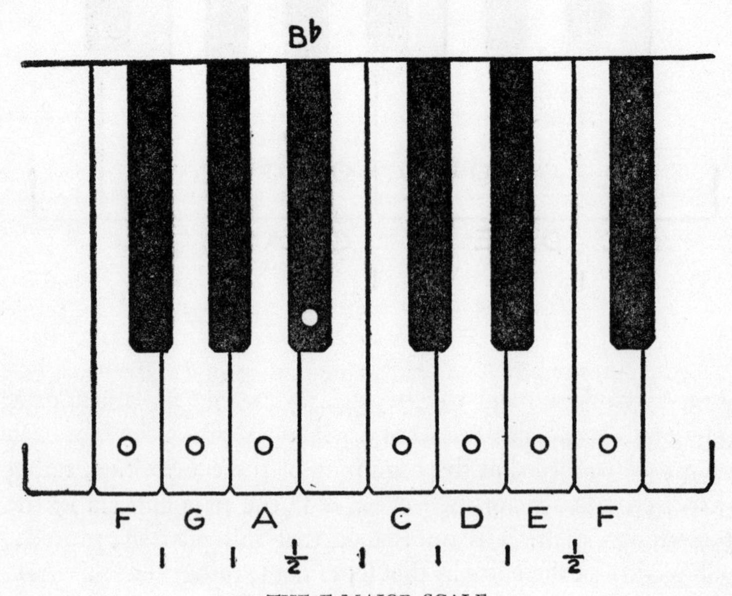

THE F-MAJOR SCALE

It would be a nice situation if the diatonic minor scale could be discussed as simply as the major scale, but unfortunately the minor scale traditionally takes any one of three distinct pattern forms. For our purposes we will chart just the beginning of the minor scale, for each pattern begins 1, 1/2, 1, 1 and this is the important part of the pattern as far as minor chord formations are concerned.

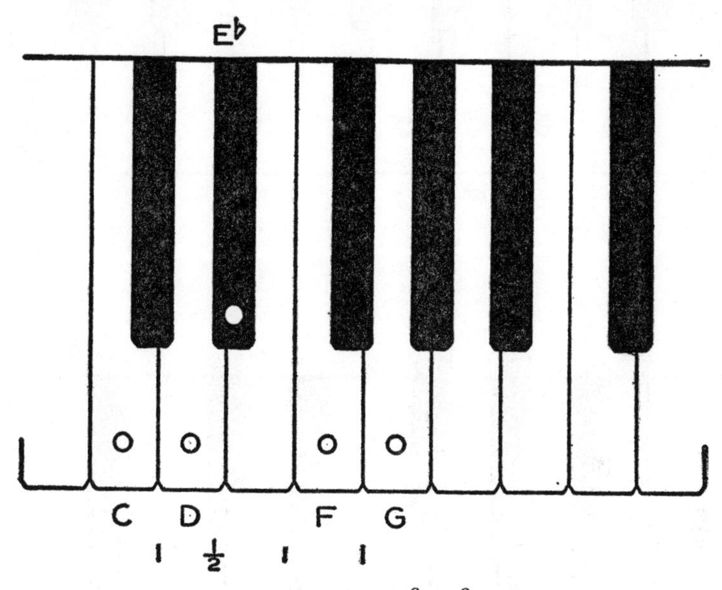


THE C-MINOR SCALE: first five notes

Using these charts for the major and minor scales, you can now figure out at the piano simple chords that will show the difference in sound between the harmonies based on the two types of diatonic scales. Playing the first, third, and fifth notes of the major scale simultaneously gives a major chord; playing the first, third, and fifth notes of the minor scale simultaneously gives a minor chord. Notice that the difference between the two lies in

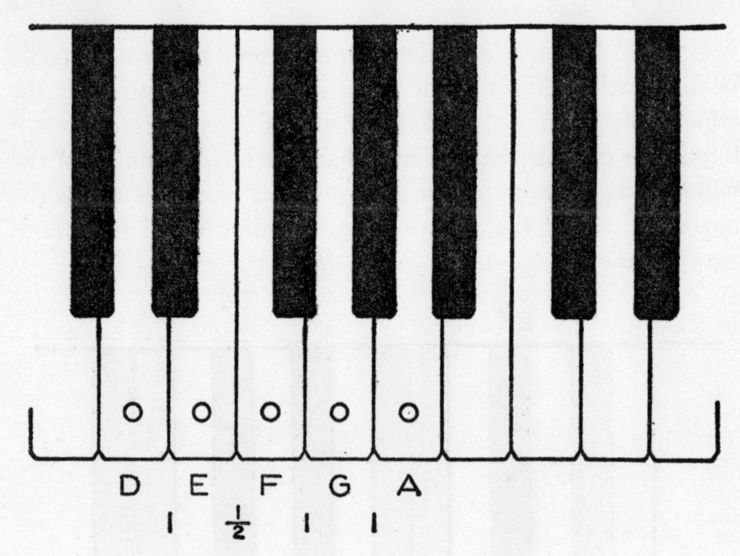


THE D-MINOR SCALE: first five notes

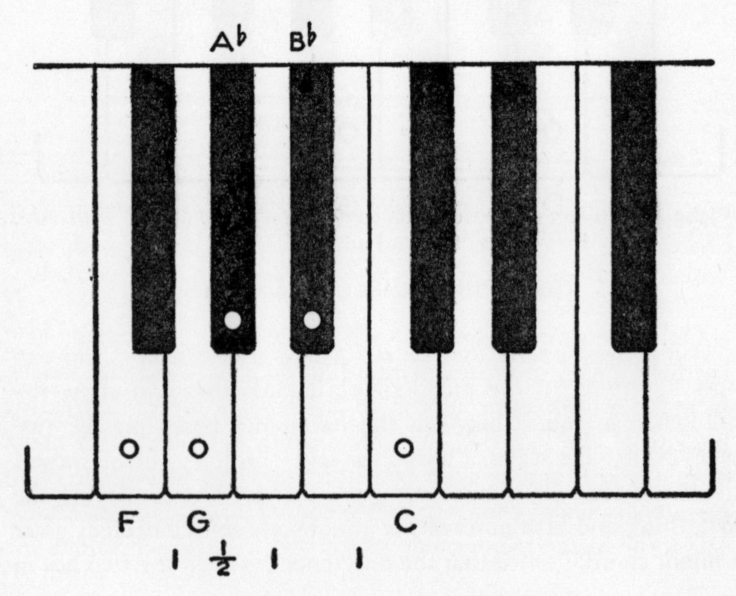


THE F-MINOR SCALE: first five notes

the position of the middle note. It should be possible after some objective listening to the two types to distinguish between major and minor even in the case of isolated chords; the characteristic difference between the two in longer passages should ultimately make itself felt.

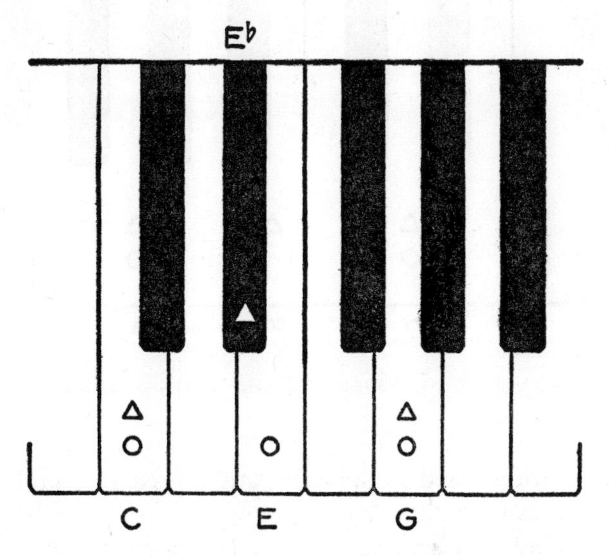


THE C-MAJOR TRIAD AND THE C-MINOR TRIAD

Piano keys to be played for the major triad are marked with small circles; those to be played for the minor triad are marked with small triangles. Note that only one tone is different in the two triads.

Only one simple chord in each of the major and minor keys has been given to represent the difference between the modes. In music a complete composition takes on an aspect or coloring because of the fact that the whole thing is written in a major or minor key, and as such will utilize a large percentage of its harmony as major chords or minor ones. The composition can be said to be in the major mode or the minor mode, depending on

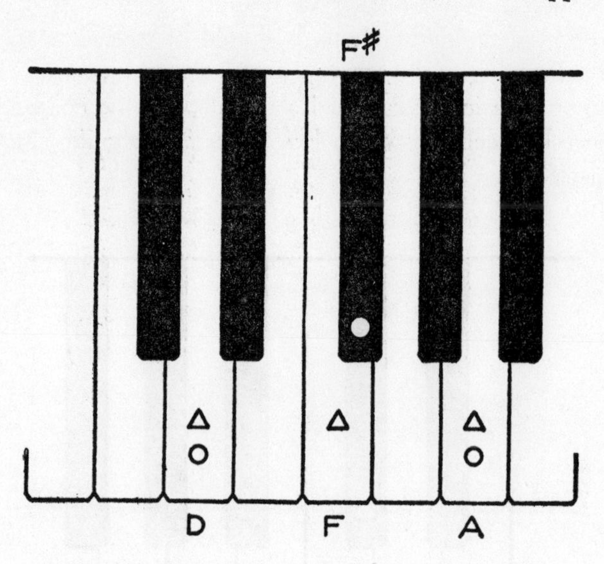


THE D-MAJOR TRIAD AND THE D-MINOR TRIAD

the predominance of either major harmony or minor harmony, which in turn is based on the scale pattern used to form the melody as well as the harmony underlying it.

Since there is this differentiation, how are these modes (or moods) used by the composer? For an answer it is necessary to generalize: the major mode is used when the composer wishes to express happiness, gaiety, a martial spirit, grandeur, or when there seems to be no reason to produce the emotional effects caused by the use of the minor; the minor mode is used to express sorrow, despondency, mystery, or to give an oriental feeling to the music. Many compositions that have no interpretation outside the field of music itself are written in the major or minor mode purely at the whim of the composer. While it is ridiculous to try to read some specific emotion into these works a recognition of the mode used should increase your enjoyment in them.

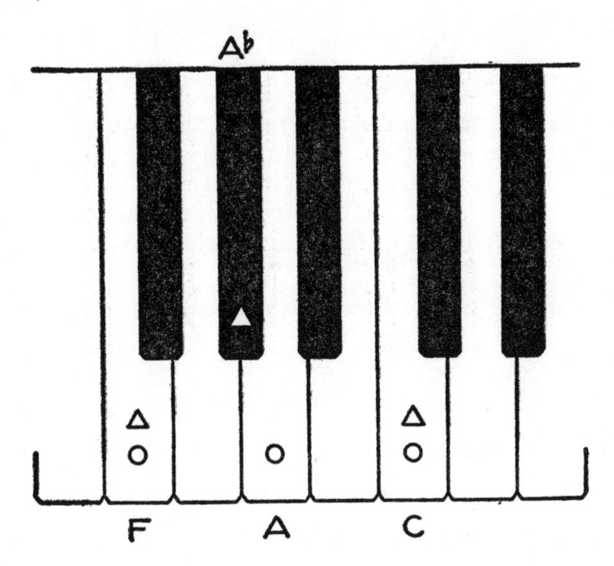


THE F-MAJOR TRIAD AND THE F-MINOR TRIAD

Be careful as you listen for major and minor as the bases for compositions that you are not influenced by the tempos, for a number may be very slow and still be in the major mode as are the two famous *Largos*, or it may be very fast and in the minor. Discriminating listening should put each of the fundamentals in its rightful place.

## *SUGGESTED LISTENING*

### *Major harmony suggested by the title*

Elgar: *Pomp and Circumstance*
Grieg: *Morning Mood*, from *Peer Gynt Suite*
Handel: *Hallelujah Chorus*, from the *Messiah*
Mendelssohn: *Wedding March*, from *Midsummer Night's Dream*
Tchaikovsky: *Waltz of the Flowers*, from *Nutcracker Suite*
Verdi: *Grand March*, from *Aïda*

### *Major harmony at the whim of the composer*

Beethoven: *Eroica Symphony*, first movement
Beethoven: *Symphony No. 5*, fourth movement
Brahms: *Symphony No. 1*, fourth movement (after introduction)
Schubert: *Unfinished Symphony*, first movement, second theme
Tchaikovsky: *Symphony No. 5*, introduction to fourth movement

### *Minor harmony suggested by the title*

Beethoven: *Eroica Symphony*, second movement, *Funeral March*
Dukas: *Sorcerer's Apprentice*
Grieg: *Ase's Death* and *In the Hall of the Mountain King*, from *Peer Gynt Suite*
Handel: *The People That Walked in Darkness*, from the *Messiah*
Saint-Saëns: *Danse Macabre*
Stainer: *March to Calvary*, from the *Crucifixion*
Tchaikovsky: *Marche Slave* (beginning)
Tchaikovsky: *Arabian Dance*, from *Nutcracker Suite*

### *Minor harmony at the whim of the composer*

Beethoven: *Symphony No. 5*, first movement
Brahms: *Symphony No. 1*, first movement
Schubert: *Unfinished Symphony*, first movement, first theme
Tchaikovsky: *Symphony No. 5*, introduction to first movement

## TEXTURE

The texture of music, like the texture of cloth, refers to the way in which the component parts are woven together to form the finished product. In our discussion of harmony only one of the two types of texture has been dealt with. This is homophonic music, which is music with one melody line, all other notes being subordinate to that melody and used only to enhance it.

A second type of musical texture, which also comes under the heading of harmony, is the polyphonic, or many-melody music, as distinguished from the one-melody homophonic texture. Harmonically, the polyphonic music is the more complex, for while the approach to homophonic music is vertical, with each note of the melody line being treated by adding complementary notes for harmony, the polyphonic approach is horizontal. The texture of polyphonic music comes about by having several melodies sounding simultaneously, these melodies weaving around so that at any given time, if the music could be stopped and the tones sustained (as can be done visually with a moving-picture projector), the notes of the various melodies would be harmonious with each other, and would actually form the notes of a chord.

The easiest way of understanding the procedures involved in polyphonic music is by using as an example the round or *Three Blind Mice* type of music. If a group is divided into four parts, and each part sings this tune starting at a different but regulated time, there will literally be four melodies (although they are identical) in progress at the same time. If, on signal, the whole group sustains the tone being sung, the notes from the four tunes would sound well together, and could be analyzed harmonically as a completely formed chord.

The round is the most simple form of polyphonic writing. The more complicated varieties are studied in a separate compartment of harmony known as counterpoint. This will be discussed in more detail in connection with those composers who were the masters of polyphonic texture. In the meantime it would be well to listen to examples of both homophonic and polyphonic music in order to be able to differentiate between the two textures.

## *SUGGESTED LISTENING*

### *Homophonic music*

Beethoven: *Symphony No. 5,* second movement
Dvořák: *From the New World Symphony,* second movement
Grieg: *Morning Mood* and *Ase's Death,* from *Peer Gynt Suite*

Handel: *He Shall Feed His Flock*, from the *Messiah*
Handel: *Ombra mai fu*, from *Xerxes*
Haydn: *Surprise Symphony*, third movement
Mendelssohn: *Nocturne*, from *Midsummer Night's Dream*
Mozart: *Symphony No. 40*, first movement
Prokofiev: *Classical Symphony*, third movement
Saint-Saëns: *The Swan*, from *Carnival of the Animals*
Schubert: *Gretchen am Spinnrade*
Schubert: *Unfinished Symphony*, first movement
Strauss: *Der Rosenkavalier Waltzes*
Tchaikovsky: *Waltz of the Flowers*, from *Nutcracker Suite*

*Polyphonic music*

Bach: *Art of the Fugue*
Bach: *Goldberg Variations*
Bach: *Little Fugue in G minor*
Bloch: *Concerto Grosso* for orchestra and piano
Brahms: *German Requiem*, third movement (starting with "but the righteous souls . . ."
Handel: *Concerti Grossi*
Handel: choruses from the *Messiah*
Mozart: *Jupiter Symphony*, fourth movement (after opening measures)
Scarlatti, D.: *Cat's Fugue*
Stravinsky: *Dumbarton Oaks Concerto*
Wagner: *Prelude to Die Meistersinger* (toward the end, when the three main themes interweave)
Weinberger: The *Fugue*, from *Schwanda*

CHAPTER 8

# Form

LISTENING to a fragment of music, such as the first line of a folk song, should make us realize that even in the few measures heard there is timbre, melody, harmony, and rhythm. Form, the additional element, isn't as fundamental an element, or if you will, as elementary a fundamental as the other four. Rather it takes these musical fragments and unites them logically into a whole. It serves as the grammarian of musical art, taking the musical phrases and clauses and making sentences and paragraphs from them.

Form in music, as in other branches of art, depends to a great extent on repetition. An architect in the process of designing a public building might decide to use columns in his treatment of the façade. If so, those columns would be spaced to give balance; they would be similar in size and shape; relief from monotonous regimentation would be achieved by the treatment of the intervening space. So in music the composer uses repetition of musical ideas, with contrasting material interwoven in various ways.

Fortunately for the nontechnical listener musical repetition is based largely on melody, which is the easiest of the fundamentals to recognize. The symphony, through its component themes, has a basis of musical form, as does the sonata, the concerto, and the suite. And so does the folk song and the popular tune, based on musical phrases. In fact, if you will think through any music you know well, you will probably discover without too much trouble that some melodic repetition occurs.

In order to be able to understand the formal content of symphonies and other works of similar magnitude, which should be set as the goal, it would be wise to approach these large forms by analyzing a great many familiar shorter works such as folk songs and popular tunes. Folk music is known to all of us: otherwise it would not be considered folk music. For examples of popular music for analysis, tunes that have lasted through the years have been chosen.[1]

To chart musical form a specific procedure has had wide adoption. This consists in assigning to a complete melodic thought a letter of the alphabet in order of occurrence: each new musical thought gets a new letter; each repetition takes on the letter originally assigned. This "ABC" of music will ultimately show the definite formal patterns used by composers in certain musical situations.

Since musical notation is not familiar to some of the persons using this book, the words of the songs have been substituted to serve as examples. Sing over the tune as you read the words of the various examples given, and the melodic repetition will become apparent.

> Drink to me only with thine eyes, and I will pledge with mine; (*A complete musical thought:* A.)
> Or leave a kiss within the cup and I'll not ask for wine. (*another complete musical thought, but with a melody identical to the first; therefore another* A.)

[1] If we were to use the current hit-parade variety of any given year, it is probable that the suggested titles would be completely unknown several years later. But many popular songs have weathered the storm of indifference so common to our popular music and instead of being merely transitory have, for some reason or other, remained in the repertoire until some of them could be classed as permanent fixtures, or what the dance musician calls "standard" tunes.

> The thirst that from the soul doth rise doth ask a drink divine. (*A musically different phrase:* B.)
> But might I of Jove's nectar sup I would not change for thine.[2] (*A final thought, identical to the first, so another* A.)

Thus the complete representation of the form of *Drink to Me Only with Thine Eyes* turns out to be AABA. Notice the predominance of the A phrase. This will help to explain two things about popular music in particular. (1) When a dance orchestra plays a popular tune, it will play a minimum of three choruses. This means that the A phrase will be repeated at least nine times each time you hear the tune played. And if a tune becomes popular you may hear it over the air ten times a day. Ten times nine means that one phrase is being repeated in your hearing as much as ninety times a day, which helps to explain why popular music may stay popular for such a short time. (2) In recalling the popular tunes of years ago you might start out correctly only to find yourself lost later in the number. Since you heard the A theme three times as often as the B theme, it is perfectly natural if you do not recall the middle portion as well as you do the first phrase.

For a common type of repetition in a different order hum through the following as you read the words, thinking about the tune as you do so:

> Let me call you sweetheart, I'm in love with you. (*The first phrase:* A.)
> Let me hear you whisper that you love me, too. (*A different melody:* B.)
> Keep the lovelight glowing in your eyes so true—(*similar to the first:* A.)

[2] The words of the accepted singing version of Ben Jonson's "To Celia" differ slightly from those of the original poem.

Let me call you sweetheart, I'm in love with you.[3] (*different from both* A *and* B, *therefore* C.)

ABAC is the pattern of *Let Me Call You Sweetheart.*

Most popular music and many folk songs will be found to be in either AABA or ABAC form. To prove this statement an analysis was made of 377 popular and folk tunes chosen at random, with these results:

| | AABA | ABAC | Others |
|---|---|---|---|
| Folk Songs | 31 | 2 | 43 |
| Popular Songs | 113 | 158 | 30 |
| Totals | 144 | 160 | 73 |

Note that the large majority of popular tunes fall into either the AABA or the ABAC category. In the case of folk songs a good percentage are AABA. The reason why many folk songs do not fit into either category is that in folk music, unlike the popular tune, the verse as well as the chorus is often used to form a complete lyric thought; the song is thought of as a complete unit and therefore more than the four letters would be required in making an analysis. If just the verse or just the chorus were used, many songs falling into the "Others" column would be transferred to either AABA or ABAC. An analysis of the songs included in the "Others" group would show a predominance of AABC, AABB, ABAB, and ABCA, again showing the prevalence and importance of melodic repetition.

One more example of simple song analysis is desirable to clear up certain questions that might arise:

Believe me, if all those endearing young charms,
Which I gaze on so fondly to-day, (A).
Were to change by to-morrow, and fleet in my arms,
Like fairy-gifts fading away, (A?).

[3] Copyright, 1910, by Leo Friedman. Copyright renewed. By permission of Shawnee Press, Inc., and Shapiro, Bernstein & Co., Inc.

Thou wouldst still be adored, as this moment thou art,
  Let thy loveliness fade as it will, (B).
And around the dear ruin each wish of my heart
  Would entwine itself verdantly still. (A?).

The question marks are added at the end of the second and fourth lines because of the fact that the last few notes in those lines differ from the last few notes of the first line. But the main part of the melodies of the three lines is the same; the differences are technically a matter of cadences, or phrase endings. These endings are, as it were, musical punctuation. We might think of a (musical) semicolon at the end of the first line, and (musical) periods terminating the second and fourth lines. With only this slight modification it is reasonable to call each of the three lines A, giving us the expected AABA form for *Believe Me, If All Those Endearing Young Charms.*

The following songs are suggested for analysis. It isn't necessary to limit yourself to this group, but they should prove interesting.

*Ach! du Lieber Augustin*
*All Through the Night*
*I'm Forever Blowing Bubbles*
*Ja-da*
*Over There*
*Shine On, Harvest Moon*
*Smile, Smile, Smile* (better known as *Pack Up Your Troubles*)
*Stardust*
*Sweet Adeline*
*Tannenbaum, O Tannenbaum* (*Maryland, My Maryland*)
*Tea for Two*
*The Darktown Strutter's Ball*
*When You Wore a Tulip and I Wore a Big Red Rose*

In a formal course in music analysis considerable attention is given to such details as periods, phrases, phrase groups, cadences, and other technical aspects of the subject, but since the nature of the book makes it impossible to go into the complete details of any phase of music, it is hoped that those interested in the structure of music will avail themselves of the good texts on the subject of form for more detailed information.

In the analyses of simple songs presented above, the length of the melodic fragment for each letter designation was one-fourth of the length of the complete composition. Since most popular and folk music is either thirty-two or sixteen measures in length, the phrase length used as a basis was eight or four measures. In the analysis of larger works there is no regularity in the length of the themes, nor does the equal division basis hold true. But the assignment of a letter for each new theme is the method still to be used.

Before tackling larger compositions, it might be interesting to see how letters can be assigned, depending on the magnitude of the composition. *The Song of the Volga Boatmen* is an excellent example of this expanding relationship. The analysis will first be made using as a basis for letter designations a musical phrase of one measure (enough music for the words "Yo, heave ho" as they occur in one translation). Since the composition is twenty measures in length, the form will turn out to be AABAAABACDCD EFBAAABA, which looks far more complicated and difficult than it really is. In the case of the *Volga Boatmen* the designation for the form based on the one-measure unit can be rewritten in a slightly different way:

AABA AABA CDCDEFBA AABA

This grouping divides the song into four parts, reminiscent of the folk song analyses that have been done, although the third part is longer than the others. Using lower-case letters in place of their equivalents in the above, we may reassign the upper-case letters as follows:

| aaba | aaba | cdcdefba | aaba |
|---|---|---|---|
| A | A | B | A |

which gives us an AABA form for the complete number. And the A is now twenty seconds long as compared to a five-second a.

But we don't need to stop here! The late Albert Stoessel, American composer and conductor, used this Russian folk song as the basis for a symphonic tone poem with the same title. Although Mr. Stoessel's treatment did not have the regularity suggested here, we can make a supposition of what he might have done. We can suppose that he might have used the complete folk song, followed by an immediate repetition of the folk song; then there might be a minute or so of other Russian-sounding music, and a return to the title music again to finish the composition. This would give us a magnified AABA, with the new A representing the first minute and forty seconds of music, and the whole thing running to approximately six and a half minutes.

Theoretically we can go still farther. Someone might write a "Russian Symphony," utilizing Mr. Stoessel's complete opus as the A of one of the movements; in this case we would have a six-and-a-half minute A, rather than the previous durations of a minute and forty seconds, or twenty seconds, or five seconds. This hasn't happened, but it shows the possibilities of the bigness of this thing we call form, and should serve as a warning that we should not assign letters to too-small units when we start analyzing symphonies.

## *THE SONATA FORM*

Many musical forms have been subject to developmental changes primarily because of growth. Years of experimental composing are needed to arrive at a set formula; not only do the media of musical performance change, but composers learn from their predecessors, and then make changes they think beneficial. The *sonata form,* which is the basis of many of the longer instrumental works that are in the repertoire, went through this process, but reached a full stage of development in what is known as the Classical period. Changes have been introduced since that time, but because of its importance to the classical composers the sonata form as discussed here will be in light of its use during the classical era.

A workable definition of the sonata form would be that it is the structure of an extended instrumental composition of four or three movements, each movement having a specific form of its own. This definition requires some explanation for each of its parts.

". . . the structure . . .": The sonata form is a musical blueprint, a skeleton framework on which the composer drapes his tunes; it sets up the pattern for the repetitions of themes. The sonata form is not heard: the music composed with this form as a guide is what is heard. You do not live in an architect's blueprints of a house, but in the house built according to these blueprints.

". . . an extended instrumental composition . . .": The composers of the Classical period wrote vocal music, such as opera, oratorio, and the mass; they composed short instrumental compositions, such as overtures and fantasias. The sonata form applies only to their longer, or extended, instrumental compositions, such as the symphony and the sonata.

". . . of four or three . . .": Obviously the order of the numbers is reversed to emphasize the fact that the normal complete sonata form is in four movements, but that many compositions were reduced to three movements, still utilizing the basic concepts of the form.

". . . movements . . .": This word signifies a part of the larger work complete in itself. As the sonata form was used by the romantic composers there is often a melodic tie-up between these movements, but in the case of the classical composers the only definite relationship lies in the key signatures. In this case the first, third, and fourth movements are in the same key; the second movement is in a closely related key. The dependence, and at the same time the independence, of the movements might be clarified by comparison with the stories appearing in a magazine such as *The Saturday Evening Post.* In past years this magazine published three types of stories: (1) the short story complete in one issue; (2) the serial story, which developed a plot through a number of installments; (3) a short story complete in one issue, based on characters that appeared in similar stories in previous issues. This last kind of story was one of a series, but not part of a serial. Examples of such stories were the Des and Crunch series, Alexander Botts and the Earthworm tractor, and Tugboat Annie. Each of these stories was complete in itself and enjoyable reading by itself, but if you had become acquainted with the writer's style and characters before, each new plot or situation in which the characters were involved would bring added enjoyment. It is to this third type of story that the movements of a composition in the sonata form can be likened. You may listen to a single movement and enjoy it, but you will probably enjoy a fourth movement better, for example, if you have heard the three that precede it.

". . . each movement having a specific form of its own.": While the sonata form suggests the structure of the over-all work as defined, each of the several movements is built on a specific pattern. To analyze the larger work it is necessary to study each movement as a unit of the whole composition. The forms of these movements will be found to follow in a definite order, but with leeway for a certain amount of choice by the composer.

The statement was made that we do not hear the form, but rather hear the music composed with the form as a guide. These compositions must have names; the names given below signify in all cases that (1) the sonata form has been used, and (2) the composition is to be performed by a certain number and combination of instruments. The following list gives the names of compositions that differ only in the playing medium; they are similar in form.

*sonata:* for one or two instruments
*trio:* for three instruments
*quartet:* for four instruments
*quintet:* for five instruments
*sextet:* for six instruments
*septet:* for seven instruments
*octet:* for eight instruments
*symphony:* for a complete orchestra
*concerto:* for a complete orchestra and a solo instrument
*double concerto:* for an orchestra and two solo instruments

If you have heard the *Moonlight Sonata*, the *Surprise Symphony*, the *Emperor Concerto*, and the *Archduke Trio*, you have heard compositions in the same basic form, but performed with different media: piano, orchestra, piano and orchestra, and piano, violin, and 'cello, respectively.

In the study of form reference to architecture makes a handy comparison. For example, the various compositions based on the sonata form listed above may be likened to a row of houses that are to be built by a housing corporation. Perhaps for the sake of economy they are to be identical in size and shape and floor plan, but in order to prevent monotony different construction materials will be used. One might be of wood, another brick, a third stucco, and the fourth will be finished in native stone. They are similar in form but they do not look the same from the outside. The sonata, the quartet, and the symphony are also similar in form but do not sound the same because of the material used in their performance.

The next step in the analysis of the sonata form is to inquire into the specific forms of the individual movements. This study will be limited to the four most commonly used forms, although there are others: these four will permit us to gain an insight into most of the great music that has been composed in the sonata form. In the four-movement sonata form, as developed and used in the classical period, the movements follow a definite order, but with leeway for the composer's choice:

First movement: the *sonata-allegro form* is used.
Second movement: the composer has his choice of any form.
Third movement: the *song form and trio* is used.
Fourth movement: the composer has his choice.

An explanation of the foregoing, based again on house-building, might prove helpful. A number of persons are planning four-room houses consisting of living room, bedroom, kitchen, and bath. These rooms will be of different dimensions and will be finished with different wall surfaces. In all cases the living rooms will have plaster finishes, and the kitchens will be finished in wallboard. One builder may plaster his bedroom and bath; another may plaster his bedroom and tile the bath; a third may panel the bedroom and paper the bath. So composers will build a composition on the sonata form, in four movements, the first and third of which will have the same pattern or finish; the other two will be built according to the whim of the composer. And the movements will not be of the same size, but will differ again according to the composers' wishes.

## *SONG FORM AND TRIO*

Although *song form and trio* is not the form of the first movement, it is the first to be discussed because of a reason suggested by its title, for *song form* here means AABA, with which we are now familiar. Admittedly the phrases represented by the letters are considerably longer than those in the folk song or popular tune, but their recurrence is the same. The word *trio* in the title also means a *song form.* However, since the letters A and B have already been used to represent melodies, the second, or *trio song form,* will be labeled CCDC. Song form and trio would then be represented as AABA CCDC. But for reasons to be explained later this did not make a complete-sounding unit. So to finish the movement the original song form was replayed, giving the theoretical AABA CCDC AABA. Perhaps in the early days of actual performance the composer or the conductor found that even when this was played according to the plot letters above it was not of a magnitude to compare with the other movements in the composition. As a result additional repetitions were added in performance so that traditionally the song form and trio is correctly designed as AABA(BA)CCDC(DC)AABA (with the next to final A often omitted). When you are listening to a movement in this form on records and find that the repeated portions are not all present, it is probably because the conductor or the recording engineer has left out a repetition in order to make the music fit the space provided on the disc.

Two factors make it desirable not to end the movement with the trio portion: (1) the trio often modulates to a different key, and it is necessary to end the movement in the key in which it started, which can be done by returning to the original song form; (2) in the early history of this form, in order to make a contrast, the second song form was written for only three instruments to perform (hence the name *trio* applied to it), and it was musically sound to return to the larger group of instruments in the orchestra to finish the movement. While the tradition of writing the middle portion for only three instruments has long since died out, examination of scores or actual listening will show that this portion, while not a trio in the true sense of the word, is inclined to be played with a reduced orchestra and thus to give the same contrasting effect as the original version.

It is a far cry from the basic AABA CCDC to AABABA CCDCDC A(A)BA but it is a perfectly logical development. This is the form of third movements in the sonata form.

## *SUGGESTED LISTENING*

### *Song form and trio*

The third movement of the following:
Haydn: *Clock Symphony*
Haydn: *Military Symphony*
Haydn: *Surprise Symphony*
Mozart: *Symphony No. 39*
Mozart: *Symphony No. 40*
Mozart: *Symphony No. 41*, Jupiter
Mozart: *Quartet in D minor*, K. 421
Beethoven: *Symphony No. 3*, Eroica
Beethoven: *Symphony No. 5*

## *RONDO FORM*

The *rondo form* may be the basis of the music of the final or perhaps second movement of a composition. It is one of the easiest to recognize aurally and its letter designation is not complicated.

In this case the composer has in mind one particular melody that he thinks will bear repetition. But in order not to have a monotonous presentation by simple repetition he inserts between the various appearances of the A theme some contrasting material. This is designated by the letters ABACA, which is one of the forms it may assume. In actual practice, if this seems too lengthy, the composer may stop after the ABA; or, if too short, he may return to his original B and finish with another A. It may help you to remember the rondo form as a sort of "Dagwood sandwich," with the bread representing the A theme, and B and C being the cheese and sardines that go to make up a triple-decker.

### *SUGGESTED LISTENING*

*Rondo*

Haydn: *Quartet in C major*, Op. 133 No. 3, fourth movement
Mozart: *Concerto No. 3 for Horn in E-flat major*, third movement
Mozart: *Concerto No. 1 for Bassoon in B-flat major*, third movement
Mozart: *Eine Kleine Nachtmusik*, second movement
Mozart: *Quartet in F major for Oboe and Strings*, fourth movement
Weber: *Adagio and Rondo*

### *THEME AND VARIATIONS FORM*

The classical composer was interested in the form of his composition; at the same time he was attempting to give his potential audiences some worth-while music to listen to. Form in itself would mean nothing except to show cleverness in treatment unless the themes used were such that they would attract the listener in an original hearing and in repeated future hearings. We might consider the classical composer as a salesman, intent on selling good music made up of good melodies.

There were various ways of selling these goods; two forms of them have already been discussed. To approach the idea of *theme and variations* we might compare the selling technique with that of the *rondo* method of salesmanship. To bring the composer up to date consider him in the same light as the salesman of some such article as a vacuum cleaner. He rings the doorbell and says to the lady of the house, "Madam, I would like to show you this vacuum cleaner." When the lady replies that she is not interested, our man says, "Okay. I just thought I'd stop here and see. By the way, you have a lovely place here: nice lawn and the garden out back looks very well tended. Things look mighty well kept outside. I imagine that with so much dirt out there some gets tracked into the house. Wouldn't you like to buy this vacuum cleaner?" Again receiving a negative answer, the salesman perseveres: "Were those your children playing out front? Fine healthy looking bunch of youngsters; I sure do admire a family like this. But I have some of my own and I know how hard it is to keep things clean with an active bunch of kids around. Wouldn't you like to buy a vacuum cleaner?" And so on. This salesman would be using a rondo technique: he starts with, and returns to, the main "Wouldn't you like to buy a vacuum cleaner?" but brings in other conversational material between questions to prevent monotony. With the one question repeated again and again he would not have lasted long in his approach, nor would a composer, using just one theme without contrasting material interspersed.

Here is the same salesman using a *theme and variations* approach: "Madam, I would like to sell you this vacuum cleaner. No? But did you know our cleaner is the best on the market as proven by scientific tests, and you should have one in your home. No? You probably don't realize that each and every cleaner we sell is backed up by a foolproof guarantee; this alone makes it valuable to own. No? We don't suppose that anything will go wrong, but if it does we give free service for one year, which makes it a valuable piece of equipment to own. No? Well, I think you are wrong, for in a recent poll conducted by an uninterested and neutral firm it was found that women preferred our machine two to one over all other cleaners and I think you should have one of our products." This could continue, the same plug for his merchandise being used by the salesman, but with variations on the main theme "you should own one of our vacuum cleaners because—"

In the theme and variation approach in musical form the same sort of thing transpires. The main, or A theme is first stated; it is brought back repeatedly with just enough variation each time so that it will still be recognizable and at the same time not be monotonous repetition. Since no completely different themes occur, it is designated as A, A1, A2, A3, A4, etc.

How are the variations of the original theme conceived? Here the composer can work with the various fundamentals of music that have been studied, varying one or several of these component parts at a given time. He may change the harmony, the rhythm, the meter, the tempo, the texture, or the melody itself. As an example, consider a composition with a theme in the major key, written at a moderato tempo, 4/4 meter, march rhythm, in homophonic texture. The major key can be changed to minor; the tempo may be speeded up or slowed down; the 4/4 could be changed to 3/4 or any other meter; the regularity of the march could give way to a syncopation; the texture could have a polyphonic treatment. The melody could receive embellishments, or be transferred from the upper to the lower voice; countermelodies could be added. Or a combination of several of these factors could be done together. It can be seen that the theme and variation form offers great possibilities to the genius of a creative composer, and it actually was a favorite form for such great composers as Beethoven and Brahms. The possible number of variations is limited only by the genius of the composer; artistic works might contain a theme followed by variations numbering anywhere from just a few to thirty-two or more.

### *SUGGESTED LISTENING*

#### *Theme and variations*

Bach: *Passacaglia in C minor*
Beethoven: 12 *Variations on a Theme from Handel's Judas Maccabaeus*

Beethoven: *Symphony No.* 3, fourth movement
Beethoven: *Symphony No.* 5, second movement
Beethoven: *Symphony No.* 9, fourth movement
Brahms: *Symphony No.* 4, fourth movement
Brahms: *Variations on a Theme by Paganini*
Brahms: *Variations on a Theme by Handel*
Brahms: *Variations on a Theme by Haydn*
Cailliet: *Variations on Pop Goes the Weasel*
Dohnányi: *Variations on a Nursery Theme*
Elgar: *Enigma Variations*
Handel: *Harmonious Blacksmith*
Haydn: *Emperor Quartet*, second movement
Haydn: *Surprise Symphony*, second movement
Mozart: *Quartet in D minor*, K. 421, fourth movement
Paganini: *Caprice No.* 24
Schubert: *Quartet in D minor*, Death and the Maiden, second movement

## SONATA–ALLEGRO FORM

The *sonata-allegro* form is the most prevalent and probably most important of the various forms used for single movements in the larger sonata form. Since first movements are sonata-allegro, and since it may also be used in the second and fourth movements, it appears far more often than any other form.

At one time the term *sonata form* applied to the structure of a single movement as well as to the structure of the entire composition. This confusion has been alleviated by considering *sonata form* in reference to the whole, and using the compound term *sonata-allegro form* in reference to the structure of the single movement. The addition of the *allegro* in the terminology is logical because of the fact that this form is standard for the first movement of the sonata composition, which is written in a rapid tempo.

The sonata-allegro form gives the composer more leeway in free writing than does any of the other forms described above.

While certain rules must be followed with rather strict adherence, the whole middle portion may be treated according to the fancy of the composer. Also there may or may not be an introduction. This may account for the popularity of the form among composers; it also accounts for the fact that here it is impossible to assign letters as has been done in the other forms to help in understanding it. In this case it is necessary to use the technical jargon, but since the terms used are common words in English they will prove helpful in a descriptive way.

The outline below, to the left, gives the structure of the sonata-allegro movement in the terminology that will be used in this discussion. The outline on the right is line-for-line the same in terminology which is more often used. Reasons for the preference of terms in the first column will be given later in the discussion.

| | |
|---|---|
| (Introduction) | (Introduction) |
| Statement | Statement |
| a. First group | a. Principal theme |
| b. Second group | b. Subordinate theme |
| Development section | Fantasia section |
| Restatement | Recapitulation |
| a. First group | a. Principal theme |
| b. Second group | b. Subordinate theme |
| (Coda) | (Coda) |

The word *introduction* has been put in parentheses because it may or may not be used. In some compositions it is very important, in some it is negligible, in others it is absent. This one thing, among others, shows the reason why letter designations are not practical. If an introduction were used, it would have to be A, making the first group theme B; if it is not used the first group theme would be considered A, all of which would lead to complete confusion.

The statement contains two distinct parts: the first group theme or themes and the second group theme or themes. The older terminology suggests that only two themes are present—the principal and the subordinate—and while this is true for many works by Haydn and Mozart, it does not hold for Beethoven and later composers who may have three or more themes of importance in the statement. Then too, the term "subordinate" suggests that the theme so named is not equal in importance to the previous melody. This again is incorrect, as, for example, in the first movement of the Schubert *Unfinished Symphony*. By using the newer terminology we permit the inclusion of more than two themes and we designate them according to the order in which they occur—"first" and "second."

There is an important key relationship which helps to distinguish between the two groups. Themes in the first group are in the key of the composition; themes in the second group are in a related key. The key change is not made in the key signature, but the notes of the new key which are different appear as accidentals (sharps, flats, or naturals) each time they occur, so that the fact of a new key is readily distinguishable by trained musicians. In case there are more than two main themes in the statement the grouping of those themes is determined by this key change. Without it, it would be impossible to decide in the case of three themes whether two were in the first group and one in the second group, or vice versa. But if the key change occurs after the first theme, the last two must be considered as second-group themes; if the key change appears after the first two, they are both in the first group.

For the listener who can follow the notes of a melody, but who does not have a theoretical knowledge of music, it is still possible to find the beginning of the second group. This is done by comparison of the themes as they occur in the statement with the same themes as they are written in the restatement, for in order to have the composition end in the key in which it was begun, the second group in the restatement remains in the key of the composition. Therefore, any theme that remains the same in the restatement, but starts on a different note (generally four or five notes away from its counterpart in the earlier statement), is a second-group theme.

The development section gives complete freedom to the composer. All rules are off. He may refer in a melodic way to material that has already been introduced in one of the themes of the statement, or he may refer to several of them; he may bring in material that appeared in the introduction if he used one; he may write new material that has but little reference to anything that preceded; he may combine some or all of these. Or he may play around with rhythmic ideas or harmonic patterns from the earlier parts of the movement. His creative imagination can run its course without being hampered by any set rules. While the older term *fantasia* is defined as "a piece of instrumental music owning no restriction of formal construction, but the direct product of the composer's impulse," and as such is descriptive of the middle section of the sonata-allegro form, the term *development* seems more to the point, since it suggests the possible or probable use of earlier musical material within the movement.

To "recapitulate" means "to repeat the principal points of; . . . review briefly; sum up." The recapitulation of a debate would follow this definition, but in the sonata-allegro form this term is not honest, for in this final main section of the movement the composer does not attempt to summarize the statement or to cut it down in length. He repeats, with few changes, what has been heard in the statement, giving the same themes that have appeared in the earlier groups; he issues a restatement of the musical content. So the term *restatement* is used as more descriptive of the actuality. The main difference between the statement and the restatement, as has been noted, is the fact that in the restatement the second-group themes remain in the key signature of the composition rather than in a different key.

The final part of the outline of the sonata-allegro form is the *coda*, the parentheses again showing that it may or may not occur. Generally it does, and if so it may consist of a few measures or may be lengthened into quite a formidable portion of the movement. It may incorporate musical ideas that have occurred earlier in the movement, or it may be completely new material. In any case it is used to close the movement with a feeling of finality. In literal translation the word *coda* means "tail," and while it never reaches proportions that permit it to wag the bulk of the movement, a more complete picture seems to be made if the coda is present.

It would be helpful if it were possible to bring our friend the vacuum cleaner salesman into the picture again to help in the explanation, but the sonata-allegro form is a bit too subtle for him to use as an approach. Instead, we might think of the sonata-allegro form in terms of a talk given by an after-dinner speaker. After the meal he is presented, and, getting to his feet, launches into his speech. He may or may not start off with a story (introduction). After this start, or if time and inclination make him forgo the story, he might say, "I have been invited here today to talk to you about a certain subject. I can best do this by making two distinct points" (statement: first and second group themes). Then he will proceed to start developing these points, referring to one or both, or perhaps to the story in the introduction if he used one; he may play around with ideas suggested in one or both of his stated points; he may, goodness knows, wander completely away from the subject and go off at a tangent, bringing in other stories and perhaps forgetting to elaborate on his themes (development). Finally, glancing at his watch, he sees that the time allotted is growing short. So he says, "What I have tried to impress you with today is first so-and-so, and second so-and-so" (restatement). And finally, "Thanks for your kind attention. It was a privilege to be able to speak to you" (coda).

## *SUGGESTED LISTENING*

### *Sonata-allegro*

Beethoven: *Symphony No. 1,* first movement
Beethoven: *Symphony No. 5,* first movement
Haydn: *Surprise Symphony,* first movement
Mendelssohn: *Midsummer Night's Dream Overture*
Mozart: *Concerto No. 3 for Horn in E-flat major,* first movement
Mozart: *Quartet in D minor,* K. 421, first movement
Mozart: *Symphony No. 40,* first movement and fourth movement
Schubert: *Unfinished Symphony,* first movement and second movement

## *ABSOLUTE MUSIC AND PROGRAM MUSIC*

In the section on the sonata form reference was made to the Classical period and the fact that the composers of this period used this form to present to the audiences of that day fine melodies which were to be heard for the sake of the music itself. This leads to a discussion of the two main divisions of instrumental music based on its interpretive phase. These two divisions are known as *absolute music* (sometimes called *pure music*) and *program music.* The divisions deal with instrumental music alone, for in vocal music the words express thoughts unrelated to music per se, making it program music by definition.

*Absolute* or *pure music* is that which is written for the purpose of presenting the music as such without reference to extraneous thoughts or ideas; it is music wherein both the beauty and the interpretation of that beauty come through the music, and is not aided by any reference to events, places, persons, or ideas outside the music field. The music stands on its own value and is heard for the pure enjoyment of the sounds produced by the instrument or instruments being used in its production.

It was this type of absolute music that made up the bulk of the great compositions of both the Classical and Preclassical periods of composition; it has also been used since those times, but not to as great an extent or with as much emphasis as in the earlier periods mentioned. The titles themselves will suggest that the music is absolute, for they are most often expressed simply in musical terms. These term-titles generally suggest the form or style of the composition so that a listener is forewarned that the music he is about to hear is to be listened to for the musical worth without reference to an interpretation helped by something outside the field of music. *Sonata, symphony, quartet, concerto,* and other names signifying adherence to the *sonata form* are all cases in point, as are compositions with such titles as *fugue, toccata, étude, invention,* and similar terms used in the Preclassical and later periods.

Instrumental music that does not fall into the fields suggested above is made up of those compositions that have a definite title outside the field of music, with the music composed to give thought to the title of the work through the medium of musical sounds. This large and popular group of compositions is known as *program music.* Supposedly it is more appreciated by the listener if he has a program, or explanation of what the music is trying to depict, before he listens to it. It is doubtful if this is completely true—although it must be admitted that some music does need such an explanation to tell just what the composer is trying to get across to us—for the finest program music is just as valuable and interesting from the point of view of the music itself, without putting much stress on its program background. Program music as such flourished in the Romantic period, and was, in fact, one of the chief characteristics of that period in contrast to the Classical period which preceded it. Much music of this type continues to be written.

To get a better understanding of the field, program music can be divided into four classifications: *narrative, descriptive, imitative,* and *indefinite*. It should be understood, however, that these four types are not mutually exclusive but are somewhat dependent on each other. If you read a story, you are reading a narrative, and yet some descriptive material will be used within the work to make it a more interesting narrative: so in music the classifications will overlap. A composition is placed in one category rather than another simply because it is more one thing than the other.

The first three types of program music listed are self-explanatory. *Narrative* music tells a story through the medium of music: it tells *the* story suggested by the title. *Descriptive* music attempts to describe by musical sounds the object or scene suggested by the title. *Imitative* music tends to imitate sounds produced by either animate or inanimate objects. The fourth type, *indefinite* program music, falls under the heading of program music in that it has a definite title, but in this case the interpretation of the music in relation to that title is up to each individual listener, for the program content of the music itself is indefinite. This is a very useful category, for it lets us classify those program compositions that do not seem to fit into any one of the three more definite categories.

Although a number of compositions of these types will be suggested for listening, it would be well to examine one of each type at this point for clarification. For an example of *imitative* program music *The Flight of the Bumble Bee* will do. Rimsky-Korsakov, the composer, has written a short number that meets the requirements of the title: we can hear the bee as it flies from flower to flower. Rimsky-Korsakov might have done a better job as far as distinct imitation is concerned, perhaps by having a single note or two blown on a trumpet with a flutter tongue, but it is doubtful if he could have done a better job both in imitation of the sound of a bee plus writing fine music that stands many repeated hearings. And that is the important thing: to give us worth-while music that is also good program music.

*The Swan* by Saint-Saëns is a good example of *descriptive* music. The composer has taken the most appealing characteristic of the swan, its gracefulness, and has portrayed it by a graceful theme played by a 'cello. In addition he has written an accompaniment for the piano that suggests the ripples that would appear on the surface of a placid lake as the swan swims leisurely through the water. This is pure description, for Saint-Saëns does not try to imitate the actual sound made by a swan, which is a very unmusical honk! You can listen to this music without benefit of its title and thoroughly enjoy it as a piece of music, but it is possible and even probable that you can enjoy it more by associating it with the peaceful scene suggested by the title.

For music in the *narrative* classification the *Danse Macabre* by the same composer serves as a good example. This tells a story of the devil tuning his violin, calling out the departed spirits in a graveyard for a wild dance, and having these spirits return to the graves at dawn, since one never sees a self-respecting spook in the daylight. Like every good narrative this music has a time element, characters, atmosphere, and events. The time elapsing is from midnight to dawn, as shown by the striking of twelve at the beginning, and the crow of the rooster toward the end. The characters are the devil and the spooks of many sizes that participate in the dance. The atmosphere is spooky and the night is a wild one, as shown by the use of the minor mode and the instruments giving the effect of the wind whistling over the scene. The events have been listed: the tuning of the violin, the dance which gets wilder and wilder, the coming of dawn, and the retreat of the dancers into their graves. The narrative is there, told with clarity and details, but it depends for help on both imitative and descriptive material. The imitation is the tuning of the violin (in which a violin actually out of tune is used), the clock (harp), the rooster (oboe), the rattling bones of the dancers (xylophone). The descriptive portion contains the use of rapid woodwind and string passages to give us the feeling of the type of wild night, the waltz rhythm of the dance, and the increase in tempo of this dance theme to describe the accumulating action as the orgy continues toward its abrupt end at dawn. With the aid of the imitative and descriptive elements in the music a good narrative is presented.

*The Afternoon of a Faun* by Debussy will serve as an example of the *indefinite* type of program music. Does the composer try to imitate the sound made by a faun during an afternoon? Definitely not. Does the music describe a scene in which a faun is portrayed in his surroundings? This is doubtful. Is there a story told of the antics of a faun between the hours of twelve noon and sundown, as is done by Saint-Saëns between the hours of twelve midnight and sunup? No, this interpretation isn't correct. What then does happen—what is shown in this *Afternoon of a Faun*? The music was written to fit a poem by the French poet Mallarmé, which in itself is indefinite in character as is summed up by its final phrase, "Who knows—who cares?" Listen to the music with the title in mind, and if you get a clear-cut picture of the events of the afternoon, in either a descriptive or a story form, or if it seems to be imitative of various sounds in nature, it is perfectly all right; but if you get no clear interpretation of the music as based on the title, it is still satisfactory to you, and would also be satisfactory to M. Debussy, since he did not have any definite program in mind when he wrote the composition.

To sum up this discussion of program music, it would seem that if the title and the thoughts suggested by that title help you to enjoy the music, you should make use of this nonmusical material as you listen. But if these titular ideas confuse your listening and detract from the music itself, disregard them, for when the nonmusical content of a composition becomes more important than the music itself, the music is not strong enough to stand on the basis of good music and should be dropped out of the listening repertoire.

## *SUGGESTED LISTENING*

### *Program music*[4]

Beethoven: *Symphony No. 6*, "Pastoral"
Berlioz: *Symphonie Fantastique*
Bizet: *Carillon*, from *L'Arlésienne Suite #1*
Borodin: *On the Steppes of Central Asia*
Debussy: *Clair de lune*
Debussy: *La Mer*
Debussy: *Nocturnes: Nuages, Fêtes, Sirènes*
Debussy: *Prélude á l'Après-midi d'un faune*
Delius: *On Hearing the First Cuckoo in Spring*
Dukas: *Sorcerer's Apprentice*
Falla: *Nights in the Gardens of Spain*
Gershwin: *American in Paris*
Grieg: *Morning Mood, Ase's Death, In the Hall of the Mountain King*, from *Peer Gynt Suite*
Griffes: *White Peacock*
Grofé: *Grand Canyon Suite*
Holst: *The Planets*
Ippolitov-Ivanov: *Caucasian Sketches*
Mendelssohn: *Overture*, and *Nocturne*, from *Midsummer Night's Dream*
Mendelssohn: *Hebrides Overture*
Mendelssohn: *Spinning Song*
Mussorgsky: *A Night on Bald Mountain*
Mussorgsky: *Pictures at an Exhibition*
Prokofiev: *Lieutenant Kizhe Suite*
Ravel: *Ma Mère l'Oye*

[4] Program notes are available for most of these compositions on the record jacket.

Ravel: *Pavane pour une infante défunte*
Respighi: *Fountains of Rome*
Rimsky-Korsakov: *Scheherazade Suite*
Rimsky-Korsakov: *Flight of the Bumble Bee*
Saint-Saëns: *Carnival of the Animals*
Saint-Saëns: *Danse Macabre*
Sibelius: *Swan of Tuonela*
Sibelius: *Valse Triste*
Smetana: *Moldau*
Strauss: *Till Eulenspiegel*
Stravinsky: *Firebird Suite*
Stravinsky: *Petrouchka Suite*
Tchaikovsky: *Marche Slave*
Tchaikovsky: *1812 Overture*
Tchaikovsky: *Nutcracker Suite*
Varèse: *Ionisation*

PART III

# The Highlights of Musical History

CHAPTER 9

# The Highlights of Musical History

ONCE again we must make the statement that the purpose of this book is to act as a guide to listening. Repeatedly in previous chapters attention has been called to the obvious fact that music in all of its various branches is such a large subject, demanding so much time to master its technical basis, that it would be impossible to include more than a hint of some of those techniques in order that the student might become conversant with the fundamentals of the subject to the extent that he can listen knowingly, and can pick out the elements used in musical composition to benefit his listening on an intelligent plane. This limitation of technical details was particularly true in the sections devoted to acoustics, harmony, and form, and true to some extent in other subjects presented.

In like manner it is as impossible to give a complete history of the subject as it would be to give a complete political or social history of the world in a book designed for a one-semester course. The path of musical progress from *circa* 3000 B.C. to the present in all civilized and semicivilized countries would be a lifetime study, and one which even now is being added to by the recent findings of scholars in the field of musicology. Consider the following as an example of the splintering of the complete subject of music history, to show the vastness of the subject.

It is our purpose to present the highlights of musical history in this section of the book. But it would be possible to write a much more inclusive volume of greater length to deal with the music of Germany only, disregarding that of all other countries. This would make a semester's course that would actually only touch the highlights of German music. The next step might be a reduction of the span of years, and to base a course of the same length on the German music of the Romantic period, disregarding all German music that both preceded and followed that period. This might be accomplished with some degree of effectiveness. Again we could reduce this to a study of German operas of the Romantic period. And this in turn could be reduced to the German operas of the composer Richard Wagner. This might seem the lowest limit of reduction, but not so! One could give a semester's course on the four *Ring* operas of Wagner, or could go into still more detail with a study of the *leitmotiv* as it appears in the *Ring* operas. In fact, whole volumes have been written on this one subject, and it has actually served as a semester study within those limitations.

The most recent edition of *Grove's Dictionary of Music and Musicians* contains over eight thousand pages of information, both theoretical and historical. In his *Music in Western Civilization,* Paul Henry Lang requires 489 pages to come through the chronological approach to the time of Johann Sebastian Bach, a name which for many persons is about as far back as they go in musical history.

These two examples of the scope of the subject are not given to serve as apologies for this portion of the book. Again it should be mentioned that for those who have a special interest in any particular country or period or composer there is a wealth of scholarly material available for further study. It is the intention here merely to present some facts concerning the progress of music in civilization, to point out some of the great names you will meet in listening to records and music over the air, with certain characteristics of these composers, and to attempt to give some sort of cause-and-effect relationship between various happenings in the music field. A knowledge of these things will not make you an authority on musical history: that is not the purpose. Nor will it prove an easy step to musical culture. But the music of any period or any major composer should give you greater pleasure if you know something of its background, just as some exotic dish might prove more interesting if you knew its ingredients.

# The Preclassical Period

FOR purposes of this study the whole history of music has been divided into five large periods: the Preclassical, the Classical, the Romantic, the Impressionistic, and the Modern. These divisions would not satisfy a musicologist, who would break down some of them into smaller divisions, but again, based on the music you might expect to hear, and on a chronological approach to the subject, they will have to suffice.

## *MUSIC OF EARLY CIVILIZATIONS*

The Preclassical period as here defined will take into consideration all music written prior to the advent of the Classical period, embracing roughly a period of over four thousand years, from about 3000 B.C. to the middle of the eighteenth century. During this period music grew from the very crude but useful art to its highest stage of polyphonic development. At the beginning it is a mere tribal call, or the beating on a log with a stick; at the end it is the magnificence of contrapuntal works that have never been surpassed.

Archeologists trace the growth of a people through the methods open to them: the unearthing of ruins, the examination of early writings, pictorial and otherwise, the study of the implements and tools of early man, and, more recently, a testing of these materials for age by the use of an atomic device. With their other discoveries they have come to the conclusion that the first music in point of time, or, at least, the first music to which a fairly accurate date can be set occurred in China about three thousand years before Christ. Civilization spread westward from China, and each country that underwent a change in state from barbaric to semicivilized to civilized seemed to absorb some of the music brought to it, and to add music concepts of its own. Little of what transpired in these early civilizations had much bearing on music as we now know it, with the one exception that the various types of musical instruments in the four choirs came into being, though in a crude form. But the beginnings were there, and on these beginnings later developments led up to our present instruments.

The music of early civilizations served as a utilitarian art rather than a fine art for the people. The beating of the drums gave a rhythm for the dances, which, in turn, were used in the religious experiences of the tribe. Singing was done in unison, and was part of the worship of whatever gods they had, or it served as signals in time of war. All in all, it was exceedingly primitive, but it did give a fundamental background on which later peoples could build.

## *The Music of the Hebrews*

The earliest music which seems to have much bearing on the music we hear today was that of the Hebrews of biblical times. Several phases of their music bear mentioning.

1. The Hebrews set a style of singing for their religious worship in the temple that has had a great influence on the music of

today in two respects. First, it was a chant sung in unison by an individual or a group, and often done in an antiphonal form, with the congregation answering the musical leader in a series of leads and responses. It was melodic, with no harmony as such and a rhythm which prevailed only because of the syllabizing of the words, which were uneven. This type of singing had a remarkable counterpart in the music of the Early Christian Church, which, on its founding, followed the style of what religious music it knew—the music of the synagogue. In the second place, many of the early traditional melodies of Hebraic background have been sung continually by the Jewish people, so that at the present time we can hear melodies in Hebrew worship that are actually thousands of years old.

2. The Hebrews recognized the importance of music in their life to an extent that they trained the Levites, members of one of the tribes of Israel, as professional musicians. A tradition of musicianship was thus set up which may or may not be the answer to why such a large percentage of the performing musicians of the present and past generations have been Jewish, particularly in the field of instrumental music. The surprising ratio of Jewish performers in the major symphony orchestras and among the great virtuosi in solo performance on the violin, piano, and other instruments will be borne out with an examination of symphony personnel or a study of the great masters of instrumental performance.

3. Music in large ensembles became a part of the expected routine of Hebrew life. Biblical references suggest great numbers of both singers and instrumentalists joining together in religio-musical festivals. For instance, in I Chronicles, chapter 25, reference is made to a group of 288 persons being trained to perform on various instruments. Listed there and elsewhere we find the following instruments mentioned under each of the orchestra choirs:

strings: psaltery, harp, lyre, viol
woodwinds: flute, pipe, reed, sackbut
brass: trumpets, shofar
percussion: timbrel, cymbals, sistra, triangle, tabret, drum

It must be admitted that some of these names were those given by the translators of the original biblical accounts in the various translations of the Old Testament, but a more scientific approach to the subject, as made by Dr. Curt Sachs in *The History of Musical Instruments* shows the probability that there were some fifteen different instruments used in Israel, particularly in the time of the musician David, ranging through the various instrumental choirs and including the organ.

The Hebrews had been influenced to some extent by the music of the Egyptians, the Assyrians, and the Babylonians, but Hebrew music reached a much higher stage of development and acceptance. No doubt one important reason for the emphasis on music as an art was the fact that it was the only true art form allowed, for through the second commandment the "graven image" of sculpture and painting was against the religious law. This is also the reason the musicologists must fall back on etymology to discover the instruments in vogue during biblical times, since it was not possible to depict musicians and their instruments, which has proven a chief source of information concerning other nations of antiquity.

## *The Music of the Greeks*

The chief contributions of the Greek civilization in relation to our music was in the field of theory. Pythagoras, the venerable mathematician known to everyone who has studied plane geometry, was interested in the science of acoustics and also played a part in the development of the eight-note scale, which came into usage in the Greek culture. Prior to that time scales had been of various sizes, beginning with the pentatonic or five-note scale of the Chinese. But with Pythagoras and other Greek musicians the eight-note scale was built from two tetrachords, or groupings of four tones. While the Greek scales were built in a series of modes (which can be heard by starting on any white key of the piano, and playing eight consecutive white keys), they formed the basis of the major and minor modes discussed in the chapter on harmony. In addition, these modes are important in that the music of the Greek Orthodox Church utilized them; the Russian Orthodox Church was a branch of the Greek father-church and continued to use the Greek modal scales. And when Russian music was developed in a nationalistic way in the middle of the nineteenth century, the Russian composers used many of these same modes in much of their composition, which helped to give Russian music the sound peculiar to it.

### *The Music of Rome*

The Roman civilization as such added little to the art of music, but the Early Christian Church was responsible for great strides in musical development, from the point of view of both theoretical advancement and artistic gain.

The music of the Early Christian Church, as has been said, was borrowed from that of the earlier synagogue. The Hebrew chant gave way to a type of music known as *plain song*, which refers to a unisonal or single melody without harmony and without written rhythm. *Gregorian chant*, which is perhaps a more familiar term than plain song, is so called because it was officially sanctioned and adopted by Pope Gregory I for use in the worship of the Church.

In the field of theory, much that we know today in music writing and terminology was developed as it became expedient and desirable to write down the compositions for the church music, so that they could be sent from their place of inception to other churches and cathedrals scattered over most of Europe. For the writing of music the initial step was a series of markings placed above the words to be sung, and looking not unlike a type of present-day shorthand. While such markings, known as

THE GREAT STAFF AND ADAPTATIONS

The great staff of eleven lines is at the left. Next are the staves designated by the treble and bass clefs. To the right of these is the alto version of the C-movable clef, and to the far right the tenor version of the same clef. Notice the relationship of the treble, bass and C-movable staves to the great staff, as shown by the lines of the great staff extended across the diagram. Thus the middle line of the great staff, known commonly as *middle C,* is the added line under the *treble staff;* it is the added line above the *bass staff;* it is the middle line of the *alto staff;* it is next to the top line of the *tenor staff.* In all cases this is the same C, sounding the same pitch.

neumes, might suggest the path the voice was to follow, they could only suggest. A more definite procedure was to have the signs of some sort placed in relationship to a single line, either above or below; then, when one line proved inadequate a second and then a third were added until the number was ultimately increased to eleven, or even more. But whereas only a few lines had been inadequate it was found that the thing could be overdone, and eleven or fifteen lines proved too involved for reading purposes. The present staff of five lines was the ultimate solution, but since any five lines might have been taken from the larger staff it was necessary to place a designation at the beginning of the work to show what letter designations were to be thought of for the notes involved. These clef signs originated from the use of the letter G for the upper and F for the lower clef. Their relationship can be seen from the chart.

A third clef, known as the C-movable clef, is also used but to a lesser degree: just where it is placed on the staff shows the position of middle C. It is used primarily for writing music for the viola, but is also sometimes used for high passages on 'cello, bassoon, and trombone.

With the staves and clefs established the next phase was the actual notes to be placed thereon. Originally, words to be sung were written on the staff, which was easy reading except for the fact that the length of the notes could not be shown. Actual notation passed through centuries of development to reach the modern type of round notes, with square notes and diamond shapes being used in the process.[1]

One other contribution of Western Church music is given here as a matter of interest. A Latin hymn of the twelfth century had a melody in which the first note of each line started on a degree of the scale higher than the preceding. The words of the hymn are as follows, with the capitals put in for obvious reasons:

UT queant laxis
REsonare fibris
MIra gestorum
FAmuli tuorum

[1] It is interesting to see a type of hymnal still used by some Mennonite sects for facility in music reading: in this case each syllable of the scale, *do, re, mi,* etc., has its own note shape, which is supposed to aid in reading any single vocal part, but which becomes rather confusing if attempting to play the four parts simultaneously on an instrument.

SOLve polluti
LAbii reatum
SANcte Johannes.

The *ut* was later changed to *do* as a more singable syllable; *sol* has dropped the *l* and *san* has gone to *si* and then to *ti*; otherwise it remains the same and still is used as the basis for *solfeggio* or syllable singing.

## *SECULAR MUSIC IN EARLY EUROPE*

While the Church was responsible for most of the formalized music in Europe during the first fifteen centuries of the Christian era, there was an unorganized informal type of music growing up in various populated areas, a music that was more a part of the people than was the church music. With the development of poetic literature in various cultures came song—song in which exploits and famous deeds of valor or romance were sung by a wandering minstrel, either to his own accompaniment or to that of kindred souls, or to no accompaniment at all. The lyrics were, or came to be, traditional with a people; in like manner, the music to fit these lyrics became traditional as it was passed from one person or one generation of singers to the next. The singers were what we would consider a semiprofessional type, living precariously or well, depending upon their popularity with the landed gentry who could afford to give them food and lodging for their contributions to the entertainment of the household. Many composed their own songs and then added to their repertoire by exchanging their works with those of other minstrels.

Although there was but little organization among the groups in any locality, they are important enough to be considered according to the locale in which they lived and sang. Germany had its *Minnesinger*, southern France was the home of the *troubadours*, northern France had its *trouvères*. English minstrels were known as *scops* and *gleemen.* The chief difference in these groups depended on the location: those in the warmer climates gave emphasis to exploits of love and romance, while those in the more northern climes sang more of great adventure and feats of courage and strength.

An interesting development in German musical life was the advent of the *Meistersinger*, a name made familiar because of Wagner's opera by that title. The meistersingers were organized several hundred years after the minnesingers had flourished; the term "organized" is used advisedly, for the middle-class men, whose trades had been organized into guilds, used this same system for the meistersingers. A youth with a promising voice was accepted as an apprentice in this music guild; by dint of study and practice and the passing of certain tests, and ultimately by some creative work he received the coveted title of a mastersinger or meistersinger. This was one of the first examples outside the organized musicians of the Church where a stamp of approval was put on the field of musicianship, and because of it secular music in Germany was given an impetus that helped make that country one of the greatest musical nations of all times. Because of the training required to become a meistersinger, this guild of singers also did much to make the study and performance and creation of secular music a profession of which one did not have to be ashamed, and one to which young men of good families could give their attention without a feeling of subservience.

## *FOLK MUSIC*

Since the songs that were composed and sung by these various types of minstrels were passed on from one generation to the next, and since many of them were also learned by the general public who had an opportunity to hear them, they would fall into the class of music known as folk songs, except for those lengthy sagas that required special study and memorization to perform. Many folk songs go back centuries to their origin, while others are of more recent vintage. But since folk music had its beginnings in the period being discussed and has no limitations of dates, it would be a good place here to digress from the chronological order of musical events long enough to consider this phase of music which is of considerable importance.

A folk song has certain characteristics: (1) it is simple enough in both melody and text to become a part of the repertoire of all the people of a country; (2) it concerns the life or mores of the people in question, and is therefore a part of them; (3) its composer has long since been forgotten, because it started generations ago and has probably been passed on by rote rather than as a written composition in its early years of development.

The third point listed is open to some interpretation. Songs that satisfy the first two requirements, but whose composer is known, have sometimes become so much a part of the music of a people that they may be considered to fulfill the requirements for folk music: in this case an admission of knowledge of their authorship is made by referring to them as *composed folk songs.* The best-known examples of such music in America are the songs of Stephen Foster. Many of them are known by the average American; they are simple in melody and harmony and rhythm; their subject matter deals with certain phases of American life. In other words, they have been accepted as part of our musical heritage long enough so that they are considered real folk music. *Dixie* by Dan Emmett would fall in the same category, as would other tunes, both American and foreign. And gradually there is seeping into our common musical knowledge a whole host of other songs, such as are sung when people sing together in assemblies, and Service Club meeting, and in refreshment parlors, and on picnics. Many of these had their origin in World War I, and it is quite possible that when their copyrights have run out and they are in the public domain a future generation will think of them as folk music of the American people.

It has been stated that the music of a folk song must be simple enough to be sung easily by people vocally untrained. On this basis we in America can and do sing folk songs from England, France, Germany, Wales, Scotland, Ireland, and other countries. Perhaps the folk music of only one European country would not be considered simple to us: the Swiss, who make yodeling a part of their vocal prowess, have some songs with melodic jumps that would be hard for all of us to master; but otherwise the songs have an international simplicity.

The lyrics concern the people, which is necessary if the song is to be attractive to the people. In this respect there are a number of subclassifications that can be made. The following list, while not complete, will give some idea of the types of folk songs that are based on various phases of a people's life. The examples have been chosen from various countries to show the international acceptance.

Work songs:
- *Song of the Volga Boatmen* (Russia)
- *Levee Song (I've Been Working on the Railroad)* (United States)

Play songs:
- *London Bridge Is Falling Down* (England)
- *On the Bridge at Avignon* (France)
- *Alouette* (French Canada)

Dance songs:
- *Turkey in the Straw* (United States)
- *Irish Washerwoman* (Ireland)

Love songs:
- *Drink to Me Only with Thine Eyes* (England)
- *Believe Me, If All Those Endearing Young Charms* (Ireland)
- *Annie Laurie* (Scotland)

Lullabies:
- *All Through the Night* (Wales)
- *Rock-a-bye, Baby* (England)

War songs:
- *Men of Harlech* (Wales)
- *Over There* (United States)
- *Keep the Home Fires Burning* (England)

Festival songs:
- *O Tannenbaum* (Germany)
- *Deck the Halls* (Wales)
- *Prayer of Thanksgiving* (Holland)

Boating songs:
- *Santa Lucia* (Italy)
- *A Capital Ship* (England)

Religious songs:
- *Swing Low, Sweet Chariot* (American Negro)
- *Vesper Hymn* (Russia)

Patriotic songs:
- *Wearing of the Green* (Ireland)
- *Yankee Doodle* (England, adopted by Colonial America)

Seasonal songs:
- *Jingle Bells* (United States)
- *In the Good Old Summer Time* (United States)

Convivial songs:
- *For He's a Jolly Good Fellow* (France)
- *Hail, Hail, the Gang's All Here* (England)

Songs of sadness:
- *Old Black Joe* (United States)
- *Aloha Oe* (Hawaii)
- *Juanita* (Spain)
- *How Can I Leave Thee* (Thuringia)

Boy-girl songs:
- *O Soldier, Soldier* (England)
- *Reuben and Rachel* (England)

Work and play, love and war, songs for Sunday or for Saturday night are all included. Some few are composed; for most we know the national background. But others are truly international, with the place of origin debatable.

The folk music of the United States differs from that of most European countries for several reasons. In the first place, we are not as old a country, and since time is a factor in the developing of folk music we haven't yet got the wealth of it we might expect. Secondly, since our early settlers came from England and France and Germany and were followed by new citizens from Italy and Poland and Bohemia and Hungary and other countries, they brought their folk songs with them and were content to use them. This would explain our dearth of truly American folk music and the fact that we as a united people are familiar with folk songs of foreign origin.

Then, too, America is so big in comparison with the European neighbors, with the exception of Russia, that most of the American folk music is sectionalized: there are types of folk music in many localities in this country that cannot be considered truly nationalistic as yet because they are known primarily in only one limited area. There are the cowboy songs of the western plains, the hillbilly music of the Kentucky mountains, the creole songs of Louisiana, the songs of the great northwestern forests and those of the New England fishing coast, songs of the Pennsylvania Dutch and of the Mexicans in the southwest. Gradually these are being disseminated throughout the land, thanks largely to several persons with musical curiosity who have set for themselves the task of making a collection of these songs, and to publishers of music for public schools who have found here a great source of musical material that is truly native. Other than these sectional melodies our distinctive folk music is based on several sources: (1) songs that have arisen through our several wars (although World War II contributed but little); (2) the wealth of material arising from the souls of the American Negro; (3) a small amount of music with an American Indian background; and (4) the composed folk music of Foster and others.

## *MUSIC IN THE NETHERLANDS SCHOOL*

The composition of music, the painting of pictures, and the fruits of other fine arts flourish best when the artist of whatever type is not only permitted to create according to his own dictates, but is encouraged artistically and financially by his fellow men. A country at peace, with good economic stability and without social unrest, should therefore be more fertile for artistic productivity than would a war-torn nation.

The Netherlands of the fifteenth century was in this enviable position, with increasing wealth from shipping to foreign markets and with more desire to use this wealth for furthering things cultural. Just as foreign musicians and scientists and scholars flocked to the United States in the decades following the two World Wars when conditions in Europe became too difficult for them, so artists went to the Netherlands to accept the patronage and acclaim possible for them there.

At a time when transportation and communication were extremely slow it was an advantage to have comparatively close together a number of musicians from various countries who could exchange ideas and who could profit from the work of their fellow craftsmen. As a result, this first great geographical center to attract composers from elsewhere gave us the beginnings of a musical development that led up to the great compositions of Palestrina and Bach and Handel, for harmonic writing, particularly in the polyphonic texture, came about in this Netherlands period.

The steps were taken gradually over a long period of years, but the following were the important phases of the work. (1) To the original melody a second melody was added, paralleling it. Since the interval of a fourth or a fifth was used in this type of music, known as *organum*, it sounds extremely harsh to our ears which have been trained to accept what we consider to be more pleasant harmonic intervals, but it was at least a start in the two-part harmony. (2) A second type of two-part harmony, known as *diaphony* or *descant*, came as an improvement, for although the harsh intervals were still used the more pleasant intervals of the third and the sixth were introduced and the two parts did not run parallel.[2] (3) A third voice and then a fourth were added, giving a more complete chordal structure, but these parts were treated from the polyphonic rather than the homophonic approach. (4) The interweaving of many voices became such a test of musicianship that it was overdone to the extent that sometimes as many as sixteen separate voice parts would be used in a composition. But just as the great staff of eleven lines was finally reduced to five, so the number of voices ultimately used for the greatest polyphonic music finally was reduced to a basic four.

The names of the leaders of this Netherlands school show their varied backgrounds of England, France, Belgium, and Holland: John Dunstable (?–1453), Josquin des Prés (c.1450–1521), Guillaume Dufay (c.1400–1474), Jakob Obrecht (c.1430–1505), Orlando di Lasso (1532–1594). Di Lasso was the greatest of the group; it is interesting to note that his *Echo Song* is still a favorite composition to be sung by glee clubs and choruses.

### *Palestrina* (c.1525–1594)

WHILE THE NETHERLANDS SCHOOL was flourishing, there came a demand for musicians trained there to serve as teachers and church musicians elsewhere. As a result, the new rules and

[2] These experiments into part music had been begun even before the actual Netherlands period.

methods of polyphonic writing found their way throughout the civilized musical world of the sixteenth century, and were used by teachers and musical scholars as the basis for their works, both sacred and secular.

Giovanni Pierluigi da Palestrina, the greatest composer of church music in this period, had been taught in Rome, probably by one of the men who had been trained in the Netherlands school. He was born in a small village near Rome whose only claim to fame is the fact that the composer used the name of the town, Palestrina, in signing his compositions.

Palestrina's music was of the highest type, but he had some difficulty in having it accepted for use in the Church. At that time, traces of secular music had been permitted to creep into the music of the Mass, as written by contemporary composers, just as today strains of Tin Pan Alley tunes might be found subtly woven into very solemn liturgical music. To combat this excessiveness church music had been limited to the nonharmonized plain song, and polyphonic works were not welcomed. However, when Palestrina dedicated a Mass to Pope Marcellus, he was given a hearing, and this work and other compositions—both his and of other composers—were accepted by the Church and became the pattern for the Mass of future composers.

## *THE MUSIC OF THE REFORMATION*

Except for those who gained musical prominence as members of the meistersingers or of the lesser, unorganized minstrel groups, the great names in European music up to the sixteenth century were all connected with the Church, for here was an organized outlet for their compositions. The first great name outside this element is that of Martin Luther (1483–1546).

Luther was not only a religious leader, but one who contributed to the musical life and the future of music in his native

Germany not only by composing some music for use in the worship service, but by establishing the type of music to be used in the services and the methods of its use. As the Early Christian Church had used music from the synagogue, so Martin Luther continued to use parts of the music of the Mass in his services. But his greatest contribution was stressing congregational singing in German rather than in the Latin in which the Catholic service was conducted. The *chorale,* or Lutheran Church hymn-tune, came into being for congregational use as a dignified, metric, four-part song. It was sung by the choir and the congregation, who could master the language as well as the vocal line. The influence on Germany's future musical greatness can be seen, for again, as in the case of the meistersingers, here was an opportunity for participation by the average German churchgoer. The chorales also were used in later years as the bases of many fine organ compositions, particularly from the pen of the great Bach.

For an example of the actual musical contribution of Martin Luther we suggest you look up *Ein' Feste Burg,* which is published in all Lutheran hymnals and in those of many other Protestant denominations as well. Other Germans turned to this type of composition, but Luther's name can stand as a fine example of the group.

## *THE CONTRIBUTIONS OF ENGLAND*

England has seldom been a leader in the composition of music, even though there have been and are a few great composers who were either English-born or who were claimed by that country. But one of the finest periods of English music, when it did not have to bow to any other nation, was in the sixteenth and seventeenth centuries.

During those years English composers came to the fore as

*Courtesy of The Metropolitan Museum of Art*

*WOMEN MUSICIANS. Tomb of Nakht, Thebes. This Egyptian wall painting shows three primitive stringed instruments and the double flute of the early* PRECLASSICAL PERIOD.

*Alinari*

*THE TEMPLE OF HERA, Paestum. (above) Harmony and form, balance among the parts and unity in the whole, as in this Greek temple, are basic to* THE CLASSICAL PERIOD.

*THE VISION OF ST. IGNATIUS by Andrea Pozzo. S. Ignazio, Rome. (left) This spectacular ceiling decoration epitomizes the surging splendor of* THE BAROQUE PERIOD.

*Courtesy of The Metropolitan Museum of Art*

*THE ABDUCTION OF REBECCA by Eugène Delacroix. The dramatic story told here typifies the expressive freedom and intense emotionalism of* THE ROMANTIC PERIOD.

*Courtesy of The Metropolitan Museum of Art*

*VETHEUIL by Claude Monet. To create a mood, to arouse a vague feeling of the whole, rather than to render any one part in detail, as in this painting of Vetheuil, seen from far across the water, was the first aim of* THE IMPRESSIONISTIC PERIOD.

*Courtesy of The Museum of Modern Art, New York*
*Inter-American Fund*

*LISTEN TO LIVING by Matta. (above) Voicing a new idea, using completely new methods and an entirely new palette are basic characteristics of* THE MODERN PERIOD.

*UNIQUE FORMS OF CONTINUITY IN SPACE by Umberto Boccioni. (right) Here again, the essential qualities of an idea, expressed in a new medium, bespeak* THE MODERN PERIOD.

*Courtesy of The Museum of Modern Art, New York*
*Acquired through the Lillie P. Bliss Bequest*

*Courtesy of the Artist*

*FASCINATING RHYTHM by Constantin Alajálov. This illustration made for a collection of George Gershwin songs throbs with the rhythmic beat and swing of* THE JAZZ AGE.

writers of vocal music, largely secular in character, and largely made up of short part songs. Of the various types of songs of this character the most important was the *madrigal*, which stemmed from Italy but which had excellent treatment at the hands of the English composer. It was written for four-, five-, or six-voice parts, each part to be sung by an individual rather than a group. Each voice part might have its own melody line or might simply add to the harmonic whole so that both polyphonic and homophonic textures were used, with the emphasis on the polyphonic. The fact that the lyric stanzas compared in interest to the music has kept this type of song from passing into oblivion: in recent years there has been a new and widespread interest in the singing of madrigals and similar works from this period by small musical groups, both in schools and professional. Songs by such composers as William Byrd (c.1542–1623), Thomas Morley (1557–c.1603), John Dowland (1563–1626), Orlando Gibbons (1583–1625), and Thomas Weelkes (?–1623) are still in fairly common use.

The greatest of the English composers of early years comes in the next century as a sort of culmination to the types of vocal music started and carried on by other lesser names. Henry Purcell (1659–1695) not only wrote songs and madrigals, but was a prolific composer of music for plays, and for the Anglican Church.

## EARLY DRAMATIC MUSIC

With the advent of the seventeenth century came the rise of the oratorio and the beginnings of opera. There had already been a mingling of the two sister arts of dramatics and music: previous to the Greek culture, music, drama, and the dance had been intermingled as a part of worship and in entertainment, and in Greece the theater had used a singing chorus as an aid to dramatization. Throughout the Middle Ages the Church had also used music as a handmaiden of drama in presenting storied action depicting allegorical truths, happenings in the life of Christ, or events in the lives of the saints, known as morality, miracle, and mystery plays. These church dramas took place in that part of the church known architecturally as the oratory (Italian: *oratorio*), from which the name of the religious musical dramas stems.

Oratorio and opera had this common background, but they differ in several respects: (1) Oratorio is based on religious stories, generally directly from a biblical source; opera plots are non-religious.[3] (2) Oratorio is composed to be sung as a concert performance; opera is to be produced as a play, with staging, costumes, action, and those other things necessary in dramatic production. (3) From a combination of the first two points it can be seen that opera is for the theater while oratorio is to be sung in a concert hall or in the church itself.

Italy was the birthplace of opera, with one Jacopo Peri (1561–1633) considered its originator when he set to music the Greek tragedy *Euridice* on commission from Henry IV of France at the time of his marriage to Maria de Medici. The work was a public success in 1600, and from that time on operatic composition became the chief form of musical expression in Italy, with church music and instrumental music gradually becoming secondary in importance.

While Peri is considered the founder of opera, Claudio Monteverdi (1567–1643) can rightfully be called the "Pioneer of the Opera." In America we may have lost sight of the very first

[3] In such an exception as *Samson and Delilah*, which was originally conceived as an oratorio, Saint-Saëns treats the biblical story more from its historical than from its moral aspect.

intrepid individual to go west, but we honor those pioneers who followed and who established themselves and developed the country. So it was with Monteverdi: he took what Peri had started in a crude way, and, based on his experience as a violinist and composer of madrigals, changed and expanded the new medium of musical expression into something far more worthwhile. He was so successful that as early as 1637 an opera house, the Teatro San Cassiano, was built in Florence specifically for mounting this new type of musical entertainment.

Although the earliest Italian operas still given performance in their entirety were not written until the early nineteenth century, it should not be supposed that there was any dearth of operatic composition in Italy in the intervening years. Quite the opposite was true, but unfortunately while much of the music composed for these works was good, the drama was so artificial that it does not stand up under actual stage production. As a result we have today many excerpts from these works of such musical worth that they can be taken out of the whole and used independently in recital performances. The two most representative names of this period are Alessandro Scarlatti (1659–1725) and Giovanni Battista Pergolesi (1710–1736).

The style of the Italian opera dominated the whole opera field until the nineteenth century, with the exception of a type of musical drama developed in France and known as the ballet-opera because of its background of ballet to which more and more vocal music was added until the singing became a major part of the work. Jean-Baptiste Lully (1632–1687) and Jean-Philippe Rameau (1683–1764) are the most important names in this field of composition. German opera comes later, for those great German composers who wrote opera before the time of Weber were content to write in the Italian style—and in the Italian language to a large degree.

## *THE DEVELOPMENT OF STRING PERFORMANCE*

Although operatic composition became the chief concern of many Italian composers, Italy had much to do with the perfection not only of the stringed instruments, but of string performance as well. Just as the Amati family and individuals trained by them had been responsible for the great strides toward perfection of the violin and its lower-pitched relatives, so the Italian musicians of the seventeenth and eighteenth centuries contributed to string literature and to the perfection of techniques necessary to perform this literature. Many composers wrote for strings and helped establish the string choir as the core of the complete orchestra. String music took the form of solos or chamber ensembles; the *concerto grosso* in which a small group of strings was contrasted with a larger group became a fine example of polyphonic writing. The leaders in this field were Arcangelo Corelli (1653–1713), Antonio Vivaldi (c.1675–1741), and Giuseppe Tartini (1692–1770): their compositions are still both important and popular in string literature.

## *THE GREAT GENIUSES OF THE BAROQUE PERIOD*

The Preclassical period, which began with early civilization and came through the Middle Ages, and the Renaissance, terminates with the Baroque era, when all art was spectacular, elaborate, and grandiose. This final period extends to the middle of the eighteenth century and, as far as music is concerned, terminates with the deaths of Johann Sebastian Bach in 1750 and George Frederick Handel in 1759. Between them these two great geniuses reached the musical heights in all forms of composition extant in their day; they should not be considered as competitors, but rather as two outstanding composers whose works complemented each other, and who thereby left us the greatest examples of the various types of music of their age.

## *Johann Sebastian Bach* (1685–1750)

IF A POLL were to be taken among musicians, to find their opinion of the greatest genius of all time in the field of composition, it is quite likely that the overwhelming majority of first-place votes would be given to Johann Sebastian Bach. Born in the German town of Eisenach, he was one of the fifth generation of seven generations of the same family who were important enough to have their names included in *Grove's Dictionary of Music and Musicians*. Four generations of ancestors who were recognized as the leading musicians of their time in their respective home towns led up to his mighty works, and several of his sons and grandsons carried on quite creditably, although overshadowed by his genius.

Protestant Germany had established an office of *Kapellmeister* in each town, a post that was sought after because of its security and the honor connected with it. The *Kapellmeister* was in charge of the music of the Lutheran Church, and such secular music as might be desired; the office was a government post, since Lutheranism had been accepted as the State religion. The position carried with it not only the duties of organist and choir director, but the implication that the incumbent should compose works for the service. Bach was prolific in his composing, but since he did not have a chance to travel very far during his lifetime, he was valued by his contemporaries chiefly as a great performer on the organ; little was said in his own time about his genius as a composer. It has taken later generations, beginning with the composer Mendelssohn, to unearth his works and to bring to them the attention and almost reverence due them.

Bach held three positions during his career, each one having an influence on the type of music he wrote at that time, for in each position he was influenced by the job he held and the preferences of his benefactor. His first position at Weimar was that of organist: during this period he composed much of his great organ music. Following this was a sojourn of six years under the sponsorship of a man who was fond of secular music, and chamber music in particular: this period gives us his great contributions to the secular field. The final position in Leipzig was one that required him to take charge of the music in the churches of that city: here his great religious choral works are in the majority.

Bach wrote in almost every style of music, both secular and sacred, in vogue in his day, with the notable exception of the opera. It is difficult to single out any one field that overshadows the others; in fact, the great authorities on Bach who have studied his life and his works fail to agree on just what phase of his music represents the summit of his genius. We can only suppose that whatever be turned his attention to came out better than similar music composed by anyone else.

Bach should not be considered an innovator, but rather a perfecter of forms and styles already established. His remarkable gifts are obvious in his homophonic writing, even though he is considered the greatest genius in handling polyphonic texture. A list of the fields of composition in which he excelled would include the following:

Clavier music: suites; inventions; *The Well-Tempered Clavier*.
Organ music: fugues, with introductory material; chorale-preludes.
Orchestral music: suites; concertos.
Instrumental solos: unaccompanied sonatas.
Choral music: cantatas; Passions; Mass.

In the section on *texture* it was noted that the most complicated type of polyphonic music would be discussed when the composer who was master of writing in that style was reached. Bach was the composer, and the type of music is known as the *fugue*.

A *fugue* is basically the same thing as a round, but very much bigger and very much more complicated. It is subject to certain rules, but like the sonata-allegro form has within it a development section in which the composer can take liberties and let his genius go unconfined. To begin with, there is an exposition section in which a melody is introduced by one voice (this "voice" may be instrumental); after a certain number of measures the same melody is introduced by a second voice which, however, not as in the round, starts on a different degree of the scale. Meanwhile, the first voice carries on with its own continuing melody. Later comes a third voice and then a fourth, one of these starting on the key tone of each of the first two; the four voices weave together to form polyphonic harmony. Next comes the development section in which the composer may expand the original theme-subject by doubling the length of the notes or reduce it by half, or turn it upside down, or do any one of a number of interesting things with it. The amazing part is that throughout all of this development section there remains a conformity to good musical standards and that the whole sounds like a completely integrated work and not like a series of tunes put together as an exercise in musical knowledge. It is suggested for listening purposes that you first start listening to fugues that either are written for orchestra or that have been orchestrated, for in this way it is possible to follow each theme as it enters and continues by attending to the timbre of the particular instrument or group of instruments to which it has been given. After discovering that it is possible for the normal ear to hear four lines of melody simultaneously as an integrated whole, (which is what you do when you listen to Dixieland jazz), listen to fugues played on a piano or organ, or by a string quartet.

Other terms used in the listing of Bach's compositions should be considered from the point of view of the meaning they had in Bach's day, for many of these terms have changed in their import in later usages.

The *suite* was a series of concertized dance tunes with the basic rhythms of dances native to various countries. Such dances as the minuet, gavotte, polonaise, bourée, gigue, sarabande, courante, and allemande might appear in formalized versions; an introduction to the suite might or might not appear.

The *inventions* were two-part or three-part polyphonic music for the keyboard. (Bach called the three-part inventions *symphonies* which shows extremes in the use of a single musical term.)

*The Well-Tempered Clavier* consisted of a group of twenty-four *preludes* and *fugues*, one in each of the twelve major and twelve minor keys, to prove the advantage of using the tempered scale, which had been introduced by Andreas Werckmeister (1645–1706), to make compositions in all keys sound equally well. A second group of twenty-four was written at a later date.

The *chorale-prelude* consisted of an organ work based on the Lutheran chorale to be used in the worship service on a given day. The melody of the chorale served as the basis of the composition, but was treated to improvisations of various sorts.

The *concertos* were either of the *concerto grosso* type, or used a single instrument as the contrasting medium to the larger group of instruments.

The unaccompanied *sonatas* were written in movements, but did not adhere to the later-established sonata form. They show the technique possible on an instrument, even to fugue performance on a single violin.

The *cantatas*, of which Bach wrote 295, consisted of music for chorus and soloists with orchestra accompaniment, based on a thought from the Scriptures; they were used in the regular Sunday service or on special days of religious festivals. Similar secular cantatas by Bach were fewer in number and less significant.

Of the four *Passions* Bach is supposed to have written based on the four Gospels, the *St. Matthew* and the *St. John* are still in existence. The Passion is similar to the oratorio, with chorus, soloists, and orchestra, and is much larger in scope than the cantata.

In establishing the music of the Lutheran service Martin Luther had included parts of the Roman Catholic Mass. Bach, a Lutheran, originally wrote those parts of the Mass that were used in the Lutheran worship, and later completed the work as the *Mass in B minor*.

## *George Frederick Handel* (1685–1759)

BACH AND HANDEL should be studied together because in their own ways they reached the heights of polyphonic music. But as persons they differed in almost every respect. Handel was the only member of his family to gain musical prominence; he traveled extensively in Germany, Italy, and England, and as a composer residing in England was lionized by the populace. Bach had a great musical background, traveled but little, and received scant recognition as a composer.

Even the music differs. Someone has suggested the following, which is a good analysis: Bach wrote his polyphonic music thinking of each strand of melody and its place in the ultimate whole; Handel wrote with the bigness and majesty of his music as a goal, making each melody only something that would help to add up to this total.

Handel wrote some organ music, suites for both the harpsichord and the orchestra, and *concerti grossi*. But his greatness lay in fields in which Bach took but little interest: the opera and the oratorio. In his Italian trips Handel had had an opportunity to hear and study opera at first hand in its native land, with the natural result that when he turned his creative genius to that field he wrote in the Italian style. But like the operas of the Italian composers of his day, the dramatic content of these works was so ineffective that they are not given today in their entirety; on the other hand many of the *arias*, or song portions are very famous, and are frequently sung on recital programs.

It was in the field of oratorio that Handel reached the heights of his endeavor. He had gone to England to produce his operas, but without marked success. While there he turned his attention from opera to oratorio and met with tremendous and instantaneous approval. The *Messiah* still remains as the oratorio of all time that receives the greatest number of public performances today, either as a complete work, or in parts. It contains fine instrumental writing, beautiful solos for all voices, and some of the grandest polyphonic choruses that have ever been composed.

It is no wonder that between them Bach and Handel put a temporary finality on polyphonic structure: they said so much in such an inimitable way that those who followed were happy to be able to turn their attention to a new phase of music that was coming into existence.

# The Classical Period

BY THE middle of the eighteenth century music had advanced in construction and content in both the vocal and instrumental fields. A summary of what had transpired would show the following forms and styles in existence at that time.

- Vocal music
  - Sacred
    - Gregorian chant
    - The Catholic Mass
    - The Protestant chorale
    - Cantata
    - Oratorio
  - Secular
    - Songs for solo voices
    - Madrigals and other part songs
    - Italian opera
    - French ballet-opera
    - German Singspiel
- Instrumental
  - Keyboard music

For clavier: suite, prelude and fugue
For organ: fugue, chorale-prelude
Ensemble music
Suite
Incidental music to operas (overtures, etc.)
Concerto grosso

Why is it that new types of art appear on the scene when there seems to be an established style of writing that is quite satisfactory and popular? There are several reasons. Among the following, singly or in combination, may be found some of the factors that might have a bearing on the change from an established form.

1. A dissatisfaction with the art in vogue.
2. The discovery or invention of new materials with which to work.
3. A public demand for something different, due to changes in economic, social, or educational outlook.
4. A desire on the part of young artists to try their hand at something new in order not to have to compete with the established masters of the past or the current age.

In the transition from the polyphonic music of the Preclassical period to the homophonic music of the Classical period each of these factors can be applied with some degree of truth.

1. The Baroque style gave way to a style that was more refined and formal and rational.

2. The pianoforte came into the picture supplanting the harpsichord and clavichord of the earlier age; brass and wood-wind instruments were experimented with to give a surer tonality and more flexibility in performance of chromatic tones.

3. The rise of the middle classes created a demand for more opportunity to hear music outside the church.

4. Bach and Handel had reached such heights of perfection that there was little more to say in their fields.

As a result, the new Classicism emerged, supplanting the music of the Preclassical era. It has certain definite characteristics, the most important of which follow.

1. Form becomes the basis of compositions, particularly in the instrumental field. The sonata form and its ramifications become the basis for the many types of compositions already discussed in the chapter on *form*. Two men who had a great influence in establishing this form should be mentioned: Carl Philipp Emanuel Bach (1714–1788) and Domenico Scarlatti (1685–1757), each the son of a famous musical father. They were interested in the newly invented piano, and attempted to bring out its potentialities by writing a type of music that showed these potentialities better than the earlier types. The *sonatina* and finally the *sonata* were the results of this experimentation.

2. Homophonic music replaces the polyphonic texture to a great degree. Here again the invention of the piano plays its part, for performance on that instrument permitted the player to emphasize any note within a given phrase: the pedals and the manual action made it possible to play a melody with its own accompaniment on the keyboard and have a differentiation of volume between the two so that the melody would stand out, even if in the lower range.

3. With the improvement of the brass and woodwind instruments the orchestra as we know it today begins to take shape. The strings remain the most important choir, but the contrast in tone coloring made possible by the addition of the woodwinds and brasses changes the conception of orchestral music. Not only the inclusion of the various instruments becomes more standardized, but the actual writing for the orchestra is done, by various composers, so that the conductor can depend on an established type of score when reading a new composition for possible performance.

## *Christoph Willibald Gluck* (1714–1787)

While Haydn, Mozart, and Beethoven form the great triumvirate of classical composers, the name of Gluck should be mentioned, since his work was affected by the coming of Classicism. His great contribution to the improvement of music was in the field of opera; the title, "reformer of the opera," given to him is apt.

Gluck, a German, had gone to Paris to write and direct operas at a time when that city was becoming one of the musical capitals of Europe. An idealist, touched by the spirit of reformation and change, Gluck set about the task of changing many of the firmly set traditions of Italian opera, for the ultimate betterment of such opera. The *aria*, the *recitative*, the use of the chorus, and the orchestral background all came under his reforming spirit. He was finally successful in his attempts, even though there ensued one of the most controversial musical battles of all time, with a division of the public heatedly arguing for and standing behind either the *status quo* group or the adherents of Gluck, who felt that a change was not only desirable but necessary. Even such personages as Marie Antoinette and Benjamin Franklin (then in France) were parties to the controversy—on the side of the reforming element.

Gluck's own operas are seldom performed *in toto*, but much of the music therefrom is still heard. His great contribution to the progress of music was the fact that the changes he introduced served as a pattern for the later great composers of Italian opera.

## *Franz Joseph Haydn* (1732–1809)

Haydn stands out as the first of the great classical composers Although he was born of peasant stock in Austria, his training, initiative, and musicalness, plus the position he held and the demands of that position, brought him to the fore as the leader of the new Classicism.

Haydn spent a great part of his long adult life as an employee of the Esterhazy family. Noblemen of that period were sponsors of the arts to the extent that the most wealthy and influential had in their retinue the post of chief musician. Haydn's duties were to take care of the training and welfare of the other musicians, to conduct concerts of the orchestra or smaller groups, and to compose new works for the edification and entertainment of the household and its guests. Although Haydn did some composing on commission from other sources, most of his works were written for the Esterhazys as an expected part of his job. He composed largely in the sonata form, with 104 symphonies, 75 string quartets, 31 concertos, and many sonatas and trios. His vocal works include oratorios, of which *The Seasons* and *The Creation* are of particular importance. Although he tried his hand at opera, the results are insignificant.

Haydn's music conforms to the sonata form; though he was not the instigator of this form, he was the first composer of stature to use it in compositions of merit, not only for the piano, but for combinations of instruments as well, including the orchestra, with both the symphony and the concerto. His place in history stands not only on the great music he composed, but also on his importance as the introducer and perfecter of the classical form.

## *Wolfgang Amadeus Mozart* (1756–1791)

LIKE HAYDN, MOZART IS CONSIDERED a member of the Viennese school of classical composers; the two were contemporaries, but the comparative life span of each should be noticed, for Haydn was twenty-four when Mozart was born, and lived eighteen years after his death. Thus it can be seen that while Mozart was influenced by the work Haydn had done in bringing the sonata form to maturity, Haydn was in turn influenced by Mozart, whose greatest works were composed in time for Haydn to have a knowledge of them.

Mozart was a precocious youngster, playing and composing at an early age. His early start at composition is a benefit to posterity, since he lived only thirty-five years; thanks to this early start and to genius of the highest order he was able to produce many magnificent works in his comparatively few years. Mozart's father, Leopold, was himself a musician and he aided and encouraged his son in his musical endeavors, which, while a benefit in one sense, was probably a detriment in another, for the child was exploited to such a degree that his physique could not withstand the rigors of later life, which certainly contributed to his early death.

Mozart carried on the pattern set by Haydn, in that he composed his instrumental music primarily in the sonata form. Forty-one symphonies literally flowed from his pen, for the last three, his greatest, were written within a six-week period. He was also prolific in the field of chamber music, writing string quartets and quintets; he composed sonatas for piano and for piano and violin; his concertos were written not only with the piano as the solo instrument, but used bassoon, flute, French horn, oboe, and clarinet as the solo instrument. He wrote forty-five concertos in all.

Whereas Haydn's vocal compositions are weak, with the exception of his oratorios and some other religious music, Mozart excelled in this field. For the Church he wrote Masses, Litanies, and Vespers. But his greatest contribution is in the field of opera, a field in which he first composed at the age of ten. Almost every year thereafter saw the birth of a new opera, but it was during the last five years of his life that he composed his greatest works: *The Marriage of Figaro, Don Giovanni,* and the *Magic Flute.*

The influence of Gluck is felt in all of these operas, which had not only great music to their credit, but a story and libretto that held them together, and Mozart made the most of the possibilities afforded by the plots and the characters therein. His operas are composed in the style of the Italian opera, but he anticipated the later birth of German opera by writing at least two of them in the German language, which in itself was an innovation.

In spite of his short life he was one of the greatest of all composers as well as one of the most prolific: one measurement of the lasting popularity of his music is the fact that in the long-playing record catalogue published at the time this book was being revised the amount of space given to Mozart's compositions was almost one hundred fifteen inches, as compared with Bach, who was runner-up with one hundred eight inches, and Beethoven with seventy-seven. No other composed had a listing half as long as Mozart's!

## *Ludwig van Beethoven* (1770–1827)

Linked with the names of Haydn and Mozart in the Classical period is that of Beethoven, the third great genius of that era. Again the sonata form remains dominant in the instrumental works; symphonies, chamber music for all sorts of combinations, sonatas, and concertos make up a major portion of his works.

Beethoven was born in Bonn and like Mozart was the son of a musical father, who tried to cash in on his son's ability, with the result that Beethoven's education was largely musical, the general phases being neglected. As a result, he found it easier to express himself in music, and he used his music for that purpose. A second factor in his life was his increasing deafness; as a man of very strong and definite opinions it became more and more necessary to vent those feelings in music, when his hearing made it too difficult for normal conversation. Disappointment in his love affairs and disappointment in a nephew who was his responsibility, his love of freedom, both personal and national, and his love of nature are all manifest in the changes he made in the existing music.

Haydn and Mozart had been content to compose in the sonata form: Haydn applied the principles of that form to music in various media, and set a pattern for the future; Mozart took the completed form and wrote masterpieces within its boundaries. But Beethoven, though he started out as a follower of what the other two had done, was not content to follow their dictates as he progressed in his writings. A study of some of the major additions and alterations to the existing sonata form will show the changes he wrought in music during his lifetime.

*Symphony #1:* Like the 41st Symphony of Mozart this is also in C major, and not dissimilar to the Mozart work, although not a plagiarized composition. The two chief differences in form between the two are these: (1) in both the first and fourth movements of Beethoven's *First Symphony* the first group becomes an actual group with two distinct themes used; (2) the third movement of the Beethoven work is no longer a languid *minuet* in tempo, but is speeded up to an *allegro molto vivace.*

*Symphony #3 (The Eroica):* Six definite themes occur in the first movement, one of which first appears in the development section, and reappears in the coda. The second movement is a funeral march. The third movement is not only to be played rapidly, but is designated as a *scherzo* (a lively, joking type of writing) rather than as the standard *minuet.* Because of its lengthy development sections and the style of the second movement, the symphony requires fifty minutes' playing time as versus the 22-minute average of Haydn and Mozart.

*Symphony #5:* In addition to the multiple themes of the statements and the rapid speed of the third movement, both of which had already been introduced by Beethoven in earlier works, two other innovations appear: (1) the fourth movement is joined to the third by a musical bridge without pause, and a section of the third movement reappears in the fourth; and (2) the fourth movement breaks tradition by being in the key of C major instead of C minor, the key of the composition.

*Symphony #6 (The Pastoral)*: This becomes semiprogrammatic, with Beethoven supplying headings for each movement, such as "Cheerful impressions received on arriving in the country," "By the Brook," "Tempest and Storm," etc. And since Beethoven does not say all he wants to in four movements he simply adds a fifth movement to complete the symphony!

*Symphony #7*: The first movement has an introduction as long as some complete movements of his predecessors; the second movement is *allegretto* rather than one of the slower tempos.

*Symphony #8*: The second movement becomes an *allegretto scherzando*, and the third movement by contrast returns to a *minuet* tempo.

*Symphony #9 (The Choral)*: This major work has a performance time of sixty-five minutes, although still only four movements in length. While the composition is in D minor, meaning that it starts in that key, each of the four movements modulates into at least one other key, and the fourth movement has a variety of keys interspersed. The second movement is *molto vivace*; the third is *adagio molto e cantabile*, just reversing the standard tempos of the two inner movements. But the greatest change is in the fact that since Beethoven could not express what he wanted by the medium of the symphony orchestra alone, he adds to the orchestra in the fourth movement a quartet of vocal soloists and a chorus, who sing with orchestral aid a cantata based on the *Ode to Joy* by the German poet Schiller.

Similar changes can be found in Beethoven's other works in the sonata form: form gradually becomes not the most important part of the writing but merely a means to an end. If the established traditional form does not prove satisfactory to what Beethoven has to say, then the form is changed to coincide with Beethoven's ideas. And ideas are definitely expressed; ideas that were with the man and needed some chance for expression. When form becomes only secondary and absolute music gives place to an expression of emotions or ideas or concrete things, it is no longer classical music that is being heard, but music of the Romantic era. So it was Beethoven who served as the composer of the transition from the Classical to the Romantic period; this is his chief historical importance.

The Classical period was comparatively short, from the middle of Haydn's career when he had found his medium and had perfected the sonata form to the middle of Beethoven's career when he found that he could not work within the limits of that form. But within that period many of the greatest instrumental works for piano, quartet, and orchestra were composed. And the form has continued to serve as a model for many compositions of the Romantic and even the Modern period.

CHAPTER 12

# The Romantic Period

ROMANTICISM is not a negative affair, even though stress has been placed on the fact that form becomes secondary. But Romanticism gives an entirely new type of subjective possibility to the composer. Rousseau expressed the idea in the statement, "I am different from all men I have seen. If I am not better at least I am different." Applying this to music, we can see that each composer can now say what he wants in the way he wants to say it. He may not express it any better than it could have been expressed by the Classicists, but he had a freedom of composition that the classical composers had not.

As a part of this Romanticism, in addition to the individual expression and emotionalism possible, two other aspects appear: (1) a definite dependence upon literature, and (2) a nationalistic expression by composers of various countries. It may be noted that until this time the greatest composers mentioned in this book have been either German or Italian, and the latter largely in connection with opera. But with the advent of Romanticism other countries produced composers who gained international recognition largely through their nationalistic expression. Bohemia and Hungary, Poland, France, Russia and the Scandinavian countries, all began to contribute great music to the music of the world, and to the world of music.

The dependence on literature shows up in many ways. The most obvious are in compositions which employ words, such as the art songs and operas, but even in instrumental music, such as the romantic suite and the symphonic tone poem, the literary background is influential. As in every period, music was not alone, but went hand in hand with the other fine arts in this change of complexion. Inventions were changing the lives of people; a new social and economic order was being developed. And with the new type of life came new demands on the composers, including much more opportunity to have their works heard through public concerts. Culture was no longer for the wealthy few, but for those who were willing to look for it, which included the ever-increasing middle class of industrialists and professional people. The *virtuoso*—the performer of music as contrasted with the composer—came into being as an important person in the musical world; conducting became an art in itself rather than a mere necessity; public opinion was shaped to some degree by the advent of musical criticism and musical journalism.

Romantic music embraces such a big field of composers and countries that it will be advsiable to consider things musical by nations rather than to attempt to keep events in purely chronological order. Since, during this period Germany remains as the greatest music-producing nation, followed by France and Italy and the other countries, Germany will be treated first. With all of the many facets of musical endeavor and the tremendous number of composers writing during that period it will be necessary to confine this phase of history to only the highlights, but again it is suggested that those interested take it upon themselves to read further from some of the many excellent musical histories in print. This would prove useful if done in connection with the whole era, or with the music of one or several countries that might interest you particularly, or with the life and works of individual composers.

## *ROMANTICISM IN GERMANY*

With the impetus given by Beethoven in establishing the Romantic school of composition it is only natural that Germany continued his lead, and that at least six Germans are among the great composers of the nineteenth century who made lasting impressions on the world of music. This group not only wrote in the established forms, but introduced or brought to public importance the art song, the German romantic opera, the concert overture, the music-drama, and the arts of conducting and of musical criticism. The men in question are Weber, Schubert, Mendelssohn, Schumann, Wagner, and Brahms.

### *Carl Maria von Weber* (1786–1826)

Both Weber and Schubert were contemporaries of Beethoven, their dates of death being one year on each side of that of Beethoven. But they had caught the spirit of the times and channeled it into their musical output. Weber, brought up in the atmosphere of the theater, is chiefly noted as the originator of the German romantic opera, a type of musico-dramatic work that differs markedly from the Italian opera, which had predominated in the operatic field. From a background of the *Singspiel* (or song-play), which was the first rude type of operatic composition in German, Weber evolved an operatic style that was truly national in book and in music. For his stories he went to Teutonic folk tales that were known and loved by the German people; the plots, although filled with the supernatural, were to them quite sensible, as against the far-fetched plots of most of the Italian operas, and the librettos were written in the German language. The music, too, was understandable and appealing; much of it had a basic simplicity not unlike the folk music of the country. In fact, some of it has been accepted as folk music by the Germans through its constant repetition and long-lasting qualities. One of the chief innovations in the Weber opera is the use of the orchestra as a dramatic protagonist rather than as a mere accompaniment to the voices. All of these things are important in themselves in relation to the music that Weber composed and take on added importance as the solid foundation on which the later and greater Richard Wagner built his music-dramas.

Opera was Weber's greatest gift to the rising Romanticism. He also wrote many songs, incidental music for dramatic works, some church music, orchestral music, and piano pieces. Of his operas the best-known are *Der Freischütz, Euryanthe,* and *Oberon.*

## *Franz Schubert* (1797–1828)

Some of our most prolific writers have been able to turn out a great mass of music because of a long lifetime in which to compose. This would be true of such men as Haydn, who lived to be seventy-seven, and Verdi, who died at the age of eighty-eight. But other composers were prolific in spite of a short life span. Mozart falls in this category, as does Schubert, who died in his thirty-second year.

In spite of this short life and the fact that his formal training was largely academic in preparation for the teaching profession, he produced symphonies, overtures, chamber music, piano pieces, religious works, and over six hundred songs.

In the symphonic field, the most popular work is his *Symphony #8 in B minor*, known as the *Unfinished Symphony* because of the fact that he laid it aside after writing two complete movements and sketching out a third; it was his plan to return to it for completion but his untimely death interfered. *Symphony #7 in C major* also receives many performances, as do compositions from his other fields of endeavor.

But it is with the art song that Schubert made his name; he was not only the most prolific but also the greatest composer in this medium. The art song is an example of the close dependency of music on literature in the Romantic period. In the folk song the music and the words come into being at the same time; in the art song the composer first finds a poem that he deems will be enhanced by a musical setting. He then sets it to a melody that will bring out its emotion and meaning. But there is a third step to complete the transaction: not only is the melody helpful in furthering the dramatic content of the poem, but an accompaniment is added that will also help in the interpretation. A fine example is the Goethe poem *Der Erlkönig,* which tells of a ride of a father and his ailing son on horseback with the purpose of reaching home before the Erlking, representative of death, overtakes them. The father is anxious and solicitous concerning the son's welfare; the son in his childlike way thinks that he sees death approaching and hears him calling; the Erlking is portrayed as an enticing individual rather than as the grim reaper. Goethe has written a short masterpiece, packed with drama. In his treatment of the poetry Schubert wrote a different type of music for each of the three characters represented: timorous for the son, enticing for the Erlking, and reassuring for the father. And he has given a piano accompaniment that suggests the wildness of the night and the speed of the rider who fears being overtaken. When the song is sung by a competent artist, it is completely understandable even though sung in German: each character can be pictured as he takes up his part of the dialogue, and the result at the very end of the composition leaves no doubt in the mind of the listener as to the outcome even if he does not happen to understand "das Kind war todt."

Schubert took his poetry from the works of Shakespeare, Schiller, Goethe, and other great writers of his day and of earlier periods. In perfecting the art song he set a style that has been followed by other composers, none of whom has equalled him in this field. He is the great art song composer of all time.

## *Felix Mendelssohn* (1809–1847)

BEETHOVEN, WEBER, AND SCHUBERT died within a few years of each other. It is interesting to note that at the time of their deaths there was a whole group of younger composers, born within ten years of each other, who were reaching their maturity, and who were destined to carry on the traditions of the Romantic school of musical composition. In this group were Berlioz, Chopin, Glinka, Liszt, Schumann, Verdi, Wagner, and Mendelssohn.

Felix Mendelssohn came from a wealthy and refined home, where the arts were considered as a natural part of family life, and not something apart or out of reach. In this atmosphere the young Felix grew, with a love for music and a knack for both performing and writing it. At the age of seventeen, for instance, he composed the *Overture* to *Midsummer Night's Dream* for production with an amateur orchestra at a neighborhood theatrical performance.[1]

Throughout his compositions Mendelssohn's culture and refinement are obvious. There is nothing harsh or discordant in his music: it is pleasant; it is "nice" music. And here again we have the case of a musician of great talent who accomplished much in spite of only thirty-eight years of life.

[1] The rest of the incidental music to *Midsummer Night's Dream* was added some sixteen years later.

Mendelssohn added a new phase to orchestral literature. Up to then the music for the orchestra consisted largely of suites, symphonies, concertos, and overtures and other music incidental to opera and other dramatic works. Mendelssohn wrote a type of music that was an entity within itself, without reference to a larger work, which he unfortunately called an *overture*. It is true that it has some of the characteristics of an overture to an opera or suite, such as its length, but there the similarity ceases. As a result, and to prevent confusion, we speak of this type of work as a *concert overture*. The *Fingal's Cave Overture*, composed on a sight-seeing tour of the Hebrides Islands, is the best example of Mendelssohn's work in this particular field.

His better-known compositions include the *Italian Symphony* and the *Scotch Symphony*, other orchestral works, some organ and piano music and several fine oratorios, one of which, the *Elijah*, is second only to Handel's *Messiah* in popularity.

## *Robert Schumann* (1810–1856)

SCHUMANN'S BOYHOOD WAS GIVEN over to the study of music, but, since the father was a bookdealer, the son's outlook was also literary, and his youth was suffused with an atmosphere of culture. Both these environmental factors are of importance, for Schumann had a dual career.

First, he was a pianist of ability, and a composer. His compositions were in the main for the pianoforte, of which he was a master; he gave to them a freshness of style that differs greatly from the sonatas of Beethoven. His best work was with short compositions, and even his best-known major works for piano, such as *Papillons* and *Carnaval*, are actually collections of a number of short compositions. The sonata form was a less successful medium for him, although he did compose in that field with some success, as in his *Piano Concerto in A minor*.

Robert Schumann had a love affair with the daughter of his teacher and ultimately married her. This part of his career might be thought of as his song period, for during several years the composition of piano music gave way almost entirely to the composition of songs—love songs of a most romantic nature. These continue to appear on many song recital programs and are considered among the greatest of this type of literature.

The second phase of his career was in the field of musical journalism. In an attempt to strengthen his fingers for piano performance Schumann permanently injured one hand and had to give up his performance career. He became editor of the *Neue Zeitschrift für Musik* (*New Music Journal*) and through its pages had the opportunity of helping to bring to the attention of the music-loving public many young composers who would not have had the opportunity to advance as rapidly without his help. Brahms is an example: Schumann saw the value of the early compositions of Brahms, and through public recognition of his works and prediction of greater things to come helped Brahms to become established as a contempory composer.

## *Richard Wagner* (1813–1883)

WAGNER DOES TWO THINGS for German opera: he brings it to its highest peak, and because of this greatness almost snuffs it out of existence, for few composers who followed him were willing to compose in a field where their creations would have to bear comparison with his monumental works.

Here is a case of a one-track mind in musical pursuits. Wagner was not interested in writing songs as such, or chamber music, or religious works, or pieces for the piano or other solo instruments; and with one good exception (the *Siegfried Idyll*) his interest in orchestral writing was only in its relationship to the opera. He had a background on which to start: the background that had been the result of Weber's labors in this field. German romantic opera had been started; Wagner picked it up from where Weber left off and carried it to the ultimate. In fact Wagner was so much interested in having the complete work perfect in all its component parts that after writing his first three successful romantic operas, *The Flying Dutchman, Lohengrin,* and *Tannhäuser,* he changed the class name of his later works from *romantic opera* to *music-drama* in an attempt to show by the compound name the relative importance he gave to each element of the work—the dramatic content and the music.

In seeking perfection in this union of the two arts Wagner made many innovations. He did not change the idea of the plot, which remained in the field of legend and folk story (with the one exception of *Die Meistersinger*), but in order to have the plot expressed with dramatic force and skill he wrote his own librettos, even creating new words when those in the language did not suffice for a given situation. To make his orchestra capable of all the nuances of tone color he thought desirable he not only added to it more instruments in the various choirs, but actually invented an instrument known as the Wagnerian horn to get a more forced tone from the French horns in certain passages where he felt such was needed.

Wagner was also very precise in his staging directions: to mount a Wagnerian music-drama requires not only a big stage, but a well-equipped one, what with dragons entering snorting fire and smoke, a swan capable of drawing a boat carrying one of the actors across the stage, a blacksmith's forge on which a sword can be fashioned, a spear to be caught in mid-air, and many other supernatural effects. To make sure that the dramas were presented as he intended Wagner even built his own theater at Bayreuth where a Wagnerian festival is still an annual affair.

Weber had thought of the orchestra not only as an auxiliary accompaniment to the voices but as a dramatic unit within the whole framework. Wagner carried that idea to magnificent heights, with the result that throughout his masterpieces the orchestra is often as responsible for the dramatic content of a scene as are the singers on stage. This is why whole sections of the orchestra music can be lifted from the complete score and played in concerts as symphonic music. With just as much thought for detail Wagner wrote his overtures as a definite part of the complete work, which was not always true in Italian opera. In addition Wagner often added an overture to the third act: in the case of *Lohengrin* this third act overture is perhaps better known than the overture to the first act!

The device by which Wagner made the orchestra of such dramatic importance is known as the *leitmotiv*. (Since translation into *leading-motive* is rather meaningless, the German word is commonly used.) The leitmotiv consisted of a musical phrase which was representative of a person, an animate or inanimate object, a philosophical idea or a situation. The scoring of the leitmotiv depended upon the situation at the time: big and brassy, soft and timorous, slow or fast. Thus one leitmotiv representing a particular character could give the audience an insight into the thoughts of that character in a given situation depending on the way it was treated. By its use Wagner could predict the entrance of a person or he could recall to the listeners a thought or idea that had a bearing on the situation on stage without having the singers make reference to it. With the leitmotiv he accomplished in a very practical and artistic way what was done in the American drama of the nineties by the artificial "aside" or what is done in a somewhat better way in the movies by the flashback.

Wagner's music-dramas are so important in the repertoire of the opera house that it is necessary to mention all of them. In addition to the three romantic operas listed above Wagner composed the following: *Die Meistersinger von Nürnberg* (based on factual history of that organization, and the only nontragic work he composed); *Tristan und Isolde; Parsifal* (the quest of the Holy Grail); and *Der Ring des Niebelungen.* This last is a tetralogy based on the legends of the Nibelungen, as edited and revised by Wagner. It takes four operas to introduce, develop, and complete the story: *Das Rheingold, Die Walküre, Siegfried,* and *Götterdämmerung.* Not only are some of the characters used throughout the whole Ring, but the same leitmotivs are woven into the fabric of the music. Wagner set himself the task of writing operas far transcending anything that had been done before his time. He succeeded.

## *Johannes Brahms* (1833–1897)

THERE IS A REACTION not uncommon in each new field of art: a reaction on the part of an artist who feels that while the new things are all well and good there is still something left to be said in the style of a former mode of expression. Brahms was this type of individual, a man who, in spite of the deserved popularity of his contemporaries, tried to shut their innovations out of his composing consciousness, and tried to return to the style of writing of the Classicists who had preceded his era. He was not able to do this with complete success, any more than a member of the present generation could live a normal life without the conveniences of electricity. But in spite of the fact that Classicism per se was not for him, because of the age in which he lived, his compositions of classical construction with a veneer of romantic feeling are masterpieces. Brahms merits the title of Neoclassicist for his attempts to recapture the spirit of Beethoven and Bach, even though the resultant music could not have been written by either of those two masters. But Brahms can well be known as the third of the "three B's," because of the painstaking perfection of his music.

Brahms was a master in many musical art forms: piano music,

songs, chamber music, orchestral works, and choral music. The piano pieces are romantic in nature, and bear such titles as *Rhapsody, Ballade, Intermezzo,* and *Waltz.* Because of his complete knowledge of the sonata form and his desire to compose well in that style his quartets and quintet are the greatest to be produced since the days of the great classical composers. In the symphonic field he wrote only four symphonies, but each one is a masterpiece, and it is difficult to make comparisons among them for musical worth. He also wrote overtures for the orchestra; one that has gained much popularity is the *Academic Festival Overture,* which has a basis of German university songs and was written when Brahms received an honorary degree of Doctor of Philosophy from the University of Breslau. Brahms's four concertos also stand high in the list of contemporary performance.

His choral works include solo songs, ensemble music, and his magnificent *German Requiem.* The songs in comparison with those of Schubert are largely lyric in character rather than dramatic. He is indisputably one of the greatest composers in the whole field of music.

## *ITALIAN ROMANTICISM*

The greatest contributions of the Italian composers in the Romantic era are all in the field of opera. This might be expected because of the long background of operatic development in Italy and because of the fact that, since opera was the mainstay of Italy's musical diet, her native sons wrote music which if successful would be guaranteed performance and which would make their names household words in Italian homes, for opera in Italy is not limited to a few, but is the chief form of musical entertainment in that country, with performances available at comparatively inexpensive prices in many of the cities and towns.

Starting with the beginning of the seventeenth century, opera had flourished and had gradually improved, but it was not until the beginning of the nineteenth century that the operas that were written and produced were of enough value dramatically as well as musically to bear repetition, and to remain in the repertoire of the great opera houses of the world. The opera that came into being is of a type known as *bel canto,* which puts the emphasis on beautiful singing: in the earlier days this seemed to have been the only goal, but the nineteenth-century opera had a good libretto to back up this required emphasis on the voice.

Three early nineteenth-century contemporaries shared the distinction of having their works accepted for production by future generations of operagoers. They were Gioacchino Rossini (1792–1868), Vincenzo Bellini (1801–1835), and Gaetano Donizetti (1797–1848). All wrote in the *bel canto* style, emphasizing the voice, which is what the Italians wanted to hear. But the three differed somewhat in their styles. Rossini excelled in the *opera buffa* or comedy opera, as shown in his *Barber of Seville*; he also used the orchestra well as an accompaniment. Bellini was more lyric and less dramatic than Rossini: *Norma* is his best-known work. Donizetti was particularly adept at writing for the coloratura voice, as shown in his *Lucia di Lammermoor,* which, incidentally, is based on a story by Sir Walter Scott.

## *Giuseppe Verdi* (1813–1901)

IN THE MIDDLE of the century there appeared on the operatic scene in Italy the greatest figure in Italian opera. Giuseppe Verdi was to Italian opera what Wagner was to German opera; the two provided almost as many standard works in the opera repertoire as all other composers of their period combined.

Verdi's composing life can be divided into three parts: (1)

a continuation of the type of opera written in the past, which produced none of his major works; (2) a second period when he started to show his genius, which saw the composition of *Il Trovatore, La Traviata,* and *Rigoletto;* (3) the final period in which he had broken away from tradition to the extent of writing a through-opera, one not dedicated to success because of the solo arias, and with no pauses left for acclaim after each major aria. In this period are *Aïda, Otello*, and *Falstaff*, the last two being based on dramas of Shakespeare.

Verdi was a genius in writing melody and making the melody fit the dramatic situation. Many of his arias are as well known in Italy as are popular songs in America—better known in fact, for they do not disappear from one generation to the next. As Verdi progressed in his composing, he also became more skillful in the use of the orchestra, which had been a failing in the hands of most of his predecessors.

The one major work of Verdi that needs mentioning in addition to his operas is the *Manzoni Requiem*, a Mass written in memory of that great Italian literary figure. The *Requiem* is sincere and dedicated, even though Verdi's theatrical instinct is sometimes apparent.

### *Italian Opera after Verdi*

ALTHOUGH THEIR LIVES and their composing dates come into the twentieth century, three additional composers of Italian opera should be mentioned here to close out the subject. It is true that they lived after the advent of the impressionistic period, yet their operas are in the Romantic medium; no stretch of the imagination could class them as either impressionistic or modern.

The first of these, and the most important, is Giacomo Puccini (1858–1924), who successfully carried on the tradition of great

Italian operatic masterpieces after the reign of Verdi. Puccini had the true Italian flair for melodic writing, and even surpassed Verdi in his use of the orchestra, for he had the music-dramas of Wagner as an example of orchestral use. He also made use of the *leitmotiv* to some degree. His best-known works for the operatic stage are *La Bohème, Tosca,* and *Madame Butterfly.* Puccini's greatness is in his music, but it didn't harm him to be a good businessman as well. By the turn of the century the Metropolitan Opera Company in New York was becoming one of the outstanding opera halls, and a good future business in royalities and international goodwill could be predicted for performances given there. It was, therefore, probably not mere chance that made Puccini write either American characters or an American locale into three of his productions, *Madame Butterfly, The Girl of the Golden West* (with a book by David Belasco, the American playwright), and *Manon Lescaut.*

The other two composers to be mentioned are both of that rare class of individuals who write one hit and one hit only. Pietro Mascagni (1863–1945) composed the short opera *Cavalleria Rusticana* in 1890 and Ruggiero Leoncavallo (1858–1919) presented *I Pagliacci* two years later. Both are in a style known as *verismo* or true-to-life opera, with the scene laid in anyone's home town and the characters approximating one's next-door neighbors, rather than royalty or mythological or legendary peoples.[2] Since the two operas are comparatively short they are generally presented on the same bill at an opera house, which has earned for them the nickname of "the twins." Each is popular with singers as well as with audiences, for the solo roles are not too difficult. A night of the "twins" makes a pleasant musical evening in the grand opera tradition, and one not too taxing on a beginner at opera attendance.

[2] Puccini had used this *verismo* idea to some degree.

## *FRENCH ROMANTICISM*

The most striking figure in the development of the Romantic ideal in France was Hector Berlioz (1803–1869). Although possessing a most mediocre musical training, he had the type of mind that caused him to learn by experimentation, chiefly in the field of orchestration. He was interested in new uses for instruments alone and in combination, and was very definite in his scoring for the symphony orchestra. For example, instead of listing each specific woodwind, brass, and percussion instrument, "and strings," as has been the custom both before and since, he stipulated exactly how many first violins, second violins, etc., were necessary to play his compositions. Because of this experimenting his music often sounds theatrical; effects sometimes abound to the exclusion of good musical ideas. For this reason he is better known as an authority on the theory of orchestration[3] than as a composer. His works most often heard today include the *Symphonie Fantastique*, which, like Beethoven's *6th Symphony*, is programmatic and in five movements; *Harold in Italy*, based on Byron's *Childe Harold* and written for symphony with a solo viola; the *Roman Carnival Overture*, which was originally the overture for the third act of his opera *Benvenuto Cellini*, and excerpts from his opera *La Damnation de Faust*. Through all of these works emotional self-expression is obvious.

Other French Romanticists were particularly talented in the field of the opera. The following, while not an inclusive list, are those who are best known, either from their influence on French music or because of specific works that have become popular in operatic fare: Giacomo Meyerbeer (1791–1864), who developed the French historic opera with *Les Huguenots* and *L'Africaine*;

[3] He published a standard text on this subject.

Ambroise Thomas (1811–1896), *Mignon*; Charles Gounod (1818–1893), *Faust*, and also an excellent *St. Cecilia's Mass*; Georges Bizet (1838–1875), *Carmen*, and the two *L'Arlésienne Suites* for orchestra; Jules Massenet (1842–1912), *Manon* and *Thaïs*.

Outside the operatic field César Franck (1822–1890) is the most important of the later French Romanticists. Although a Belgian by birth he is considered as a member of the French school because of his long residence and teaching in Paris. Franck's music for no matter what medium shows the influence of his knowledge of the organ, which was his major instrument, and for which he wrote many compositions. His one *Symphony in D minor*, his oratorio *Les Béatitudes*, and his compositions for piano also show startling innovations in key relationships and chromatic harmonies. The music is filled with a kind of mysticism which might well be considered a herald of the impressionistic music that was beginning in France about the time of his death.

Camille Saint-Saëns (1835–1921) also belongs with the French Romanticists rather than with the later Impressionists. Saint-Saëns was one of a group who attempted to establish a nationalistic school of French music after the Franco-Prussian war to show that France was not dependent on German composers and German musical ideas; since a real nationalistic school is based on the use of native folk music and native ideas rather than on a negative outlook of getting away from something else, the attempt could not be considered very satisfactory or important. Saint-Saëns was one of those composers who wrote much good music but little great music. His best works include the tone poem *Danse Macabre*, the opera *Samson et Dalila*, several concertos and symphonies, and parts of a suite for orchestra and two pianos known as the *Carnival of the Animals*.

## *NATIONALISM IN MUSIC*

Before dealing with the Romantic movement in the music of the other European countries during the nineteenth century, we shall do well to take a look at the subject of nationalism, for this looms as an important part of the music of Russia, Hungary, Poland, Bohemia, and Norway. Nationalism refers to certain characteristics of the music that occur because of the composer's background and training.

Certain writers have made the statement that nationalistic music only comes when a nation feels that it must assert its artistic self. This statement is representative of one type of nationalism, but it does not go far enough into the subject. Nationalism should be divided into two categories: unconscious and deliberate. In the case of unconscious nationalism a composer writes the way he does because his birth, his training, and perhaps his love for his native land make it impossible for him to write in any other way unless he consciously sets out to do so, and even then his own nationalistic tendencies may be so deep-rooted that the results will show his nationalism whether he wills it or not.

For a case in point take Dvořák's *From the New World Symphony*. Dvořák came to the United States for a four-year stay, and while here wrote several compositions that were supposed to show his impressions and opinions of this country. In writing the symphony he tried to include ideas from and about our native Negro and Indian music, both of which had appealed to him as truly American. But except for the melody of the English horn solo in the *Largo* movement, which represented Dvořák's own idea of a Negro spiritual (and which has since received several sets of characteristic words, such as *Massa Dear* and *Goin' Home*), the entire composition sounds far more Bohemian than it does American, because of Dvořák's background and training. In a like manner the music of the Russians, particularly of "The Russian Five," sounds much more like Russian music than it does like the music of any other country, even when these composers were not attempting to impress us with Russian culture.

The second, the deliberate or conscious type of nationalism is that in which the composer willfully uses as part of a larger work either excerpts or complete compositions from his native land. He may use typical folk songs, religious music, or national patriotic tunes, and the listener who knows these tunes is led to think of the country where they originated. As a case in point, Tchaikovsky, because of his European musical training, does not necessarily sound very Russian much of the time. But on the other hand he can give us a willfully forced nationalistic reaction through his music to a greater degree than can almost any composer. In his *1812 Overture* he wants you to think of his country, so he uses a Russian folk song, one of the great compositions from the Russian Church, and to clinch matters he brings in the *Russian National Anthem*, played fortissimo on the low brasses and strings.

If you demand the obvious, you can get musical nationalism from this second or deliberate type of composing; if you are willing to absorb general ideas through repeated listenings to great works, you will find the unconscious type to be just as true a manifestation of nationalism.

Music of certain countries is easier to recognize as nationalistic than is music from certain other countries. German music, for instance, does not sound particularly German to us except in a few isolated cases, because, at least in the field of instrumental music, the German music of the great masters is the type to which we have listened either consciously or unconsciously all our lives. If you will make a list of the great German composers, you will see that they dominate the concert field. We have been brought up on their compositions, and are not likely to think that they sound very nationalistic, for we are familiar with them and with their style. Hungary, on the other hand, has not had as many outstanding composers; there is a certain characteristic wild freedom stemming from the Magyars that is different and that gives us a feeling of being different. It is this difference from the normal that causes Hungarian music to sound more nationalistic to us than does German music.

America is developing a nationalistic type of music. This stems from several sources, such as the songs written for the minstrel shows of an earlier age, which seem to have an American aspect, even though their words might not be known. More recently the music of such composers as George Gershwin and Ferde Grofé has had a definite nationalistic feel to it. Gershwin was a product of America and the popular music of America of his time: the *Rhapsody in Blue* shows this in no uncertain way. And think what Gershwin might have done if he had set out to write a *From the New World Symphony*! There would have been no confusion there about where the music came from.

## *THE ROMANTIC MUSIC OF POLAND*

Frédéric Chopin (1810–1849) was the child of a French father and a Polish mother; as so often happens in mixed marriages the son was most influenced by his maternal inheritance. It is true that he lived most of his life in Paris and some historians include him in the French school of composition, but because of his inheritance and boyhood residence enough of the Polish Romantic spirit shows in his works to place him in a class by himself as a Polish nationalist.

Chopin was a composer in only one medium: the piano. And as such he is considered the greatest composer of piano music the world has yet produced. Like Schumann he was best in the shorter forms: his sonatas are good but are not comparable to many of his other works. His piano music is truly Romantic in concept: his melodies are fluent and decorated with skill; his harmonies are satisfactory and interesting without becoming overemphatic. As a pianist he was interested in getting from the instrument all possible effects that were purely pianistic, and as such gave minute attention to the use of the several pedals, to correct fingering for his more difficult passages, and to the accompanying figures for his melodies.

Although a Romanticist, Chopin did not use many titles for his works that fall outside the music field. His compositions are grouped according to their intent, and generic titles serve for them. The Polish influence shows up most strongly in the *mazurkas* and *polonaises,* both of which were concertized versions of these two types of Polish dances. His other major works are called *ballades, études, impromptus, nocturnes, preludes,* and *waltzes.* Each group has its own form and characteristics, but there is nothing stereotyped about them.

The average piano recital audience feels somehow cheated or let down if there is not at least one group of Chopin compositions on the program, and rightfully so.

## *THE ROMANTIC MUSIC OF HUNGARY*

Just as Chopin is sometimes classed with the French Romanticists, Franz Liszt (1811–1886) is sometimes placed in the German group. He was born in Hungary, studied in Austria, lived for a time in Paris, was *Kapellmeister* in Germany, and studied for the priesthood in Rome. Possibly it would be safer to call Liszt an internationalist, but because of his birthplace and because such music as he did write with nationalistic viewpoint was Hungarian music, it is safe to classify him in that country.

Liszt was primarily a great pianist. It is unfortunate that the mechanics for reproducing music on records or tape had not been invented while he was living, for comparative skill can only be a matter of judgment. But it is conceded by many authorities that Liszt was the greatest pianist who has yet lived. The fact that he could and did play his own compositions, many of which are of the most extreme technical difficulty, is one basis of judgment.

His approach to piano composition was different from Chopin's. Liszt was not interested in the piano as a piano, but as an instrument on which to produce as much sound as might come from a full symphony orchestra. If Chopin's piano music can be considered delicate, lacy, and perhaps a bit effeminate, Liszt's is a red-blooded, full-bodied, ten-fingered masculine music. Liszt was actually so much interested in this orchestral-imitative phase of the piano that he made piano transcriptions of Beethoven symphonies, Wagner preludes, Bach organ fugues, and several hundred other works of the same magnitude. These undoubtedly were undertaken to demonstrate his skill as a piano virtuoso, but they also helped in calling to the attention of the listening public some lesser-known works.

Liszt's original piano music was not less showy and dramatic. Of his many piano works the best-known are the series of fifteen *Hungarian Rhapsodies*, in which he borrowed both ideas and actual melodies from the folk music of the Magyars. These are now performed as piano solos, piano duos, or in orchestral arrangements—all of which were done by Liszt himself.

A second contribution of Liszt was the creation of still another type of music for the orchestra known as the *symphonic tone poem*. Except for the omission of words this is similar in concept to the *art song* which was discussed in the section on Schubert. A dramatic poem or other piece of literature is chosen as the programmatic basis; an orchestral composition is written to bring out the dramatic flow of this poetry. Here again is an example of the close relationship between music and literature that was so prevalent in the Romantic era. Liszt wrote thirteen of these symphonic tone poems, based on the literature of Goethe, Schiller, Shakespeare, and others. The best-known is *Les Préludes,* with a background of *Méditations poétiques* by the French poet Lamartine.[4]

## *THE ROMANTIC MUSIC OF BOHEMIA*

Bohemia is a country that has proudly kept its customs and art forms through the years even though its political life has been one series of subjugations.[5] Perhaps it has been this endless suppression that has made the country so cognizant of its early history and so anxious to bring its culture more to the attention of the world.

Two composers stand out in its musical development; both belong to the Romantic period. They not only wrote the music they did because of love for their native land, but they utilized the melodies and harmonic structure and energetic rhythms peculiar to their people.

Bedřich Smetana (1824–1884) can be considered the founder of the nationalistic school of Bohemian music. Almost all of his music that is currently produced not only is written in a nationalistic style, but bears nationalistic titles. The two best examples are an opera, *The Bartered Bride,* and the *Moldau. The Bartered Bride* has a Bohemian village as its locale and abounds in dance and folk music for the chorus, and, as if thumbing its nose at fate, it has a happy ending. The *Moldau* is a symphonic tone poem; the Moldau River which flows through the country is traced progressively by the orchestra from its source to its mouth; again

[4] One of the most thrilling performances of this work to witness is during the closing concert of the National Music Camp at Interlochen, Michigan, each year, when the young people of the combined bands, orchestras, choirs, and ballet corps join in its performance.

[5] It is now Czechoslovakia on the map.

the melodies and rhythms of Bohemia are used most effectively.

Better known in the United States because of his residence here and because of the compositions he wrote about America is Smetana's pupil Antonín Dvořák (1841–1904). But Dvořák was no less a nationalist than was Smetana, and, as it has been said, his compositions that supposedly reflect the music of the United States are purely Bohemian in character. The two best-known of his American-written works are the *From the New World Symphony* and the *American Quartet No. 6 in F major*. A *Concerto for 'Cello* and a series of *Slavonic Dances* for orchestra also retain their popularity.

## *THE ROMANTIC MUSIC OF SCANDINAVIA*

With the rise of Romanticism and the self-expression that was such a part of it, it was natural that in every country there would be composers who would express thoughts about their land or its people in music representative of those people. While this is true, it is also true that not all of these countries were fortunate enough to bring forth a composer who would become renowned outside of the borders of his native land. For example, in the Scandinavian countries only Norway produced a composer of such stature that his works are known wherever music is sung and played.

This composer is Edvard Grieg (1843–1907). Much of his music bears titles that would immediately associate him with Norway; much of his music is written with the barren harmonic structure and the minor mode that might cause us to think of this northern country. Some songs, a *Piano Concerto in A minor*, and the two *Peer Gynt Suites* are his best-known works, the latter being written as incidental music for the play of that name by the great Norwegian author, Henrik Ibsen. Grieg arose to greatness only rarely, but he remains the best example of the nationalistic trend in Scandinavia.

## *THE ROMANTIC MUSIC OF RUSSIA*

Russian culture in the early nineteenth century had an odd interpretation. Its rulers and wealthy class wanted to be considered a cultured people, and were so in their own eyes. But their idea of culture was that it must be absorbed from without, that nothing composed in Russia was of value. As a result, St. Petersburg and Moscow heard the greatest in music produced by the greatest artists, by hiring symphony orchestras and opera companies to come from Italy and France and Germany and produce the great masterpieces of music for them. They failed to realize that within Russia itself there were composers of some genius who might have equaled the musical production of any other nation had they only been given an opportunity to have their works played and sung and heard.

But these composers had had as the sole outlet for their works the Russian Orthodox Church, which became, as a result, one of the great storehouses of music in that country. An examination of church music will reveal how many fine anthems by Russian composers have been adapted to the Protestant service from the Russian Orthodox liturgy. When it finally became possible for Russian composers to be heard in the fields of opera and symphony and song, this church music was one of the two nationalistic bases that served as a supply of material. It has helped to give a different sound to the Russian romantic music, for the Russian Church retained the modes of the Greek Church, and modal music is different from that based on the more common major and minor scales.

The second treasury from which the composers could borrow was the great mass of folk music in Russia. That country, like the United States, is so large that various types of folk music existed in its various sections. Much of it, for instance, has a definite oriental feeling, since Russia is not only European but Asiatic as well. Folk music and church music, therefore, were great untapped sources of musical material until about the middle of the nineteenth century.

The first Russian composer to gain recognition both in Russia and elsewhere was Mikhail Glinka (1803–1857). Like Weber and Smetana and the French and Italian Romanticists, and like the other great Russians to follow him, Glinka realized that opera was a good medium for nationalism in that it could use not only its own musical pattern, but could emphasize its national thought by using a native story. As a result, his best contributions are the two operas, *A Life for the Tsar* and *Russlan and Ludmila.*

### *The Russian Five*

FOLLOWING THE LEAD and success of Glinka more Russian composers became interested in the composition of secular music. Five of these banded together in what is one of the most remarkable projects in all music history, for musical geniuses are often of such a type of personality that it is fortunate if any two of them can see eye to eye on musical matters and can live together in an amicable way. And here were no less than five men of varying degrees of genius, who were so intent upon the promotion of Russian music as a force in the musical world that they were able to forget their differences and work together for the common goal.

Two of these, Mily Alexeyevich Balakirev (1837–1910), who was the only professionally trained musician in the group when it was organized, and César Cui (1835–1918), who had been trained as a professor of military engineering, are of such minor importance that they are mentioned here only as a matter of historical interest. But the other three made a lasting impression on the music of Russia, and thereby on the music of the world.

Alexander Borodin (1834–1887) had established a successful career as a professor of organic chemistry and doctor of medicine and for spare-time relaxation played the piano and 'cello with some facility. But his interest in music was such that he became one of The Russian Five under the guidance of Balakirev. In what time he had he mastered the study of harmony and orchestration, and proceeded to compose the opera *Prince Igor*, which included folk melodies in the well-known ballet section entitled the *Polovetzian Dances*;[6] two symphonies, the second of which borrows melodies already used in his opera, and which is written in a strict sonata form; some songs and chamber music; and the orchestral tone poem *On the Steppes of Central Asia*. These compositions made Dr. Borodin one of the great figures in Russian music, which is remarkable because of his late start and the fact that he did not give up his scientific career at any time.

Modest Mussorgsky (or Moussorgsky)[7] (1839–1881) had studied the piano during his boyhood, as so many study the piano, but the thought of becoming a professional musician did not make itself felt until he was in early manhood. At that time he resigned from his army career, with the thought of turning full attention to composition, in spite of the fact that other members of The Five were carrying on dual careers. The musical life not proving financially remunerative, he took a government post to help pay his expenses while composing.

Mussorgsky is the most Russian-sounding of The Russian Five; his music is unmistakably nationalistic. An almost barren and pagan crudity may be explained by the fact that he had but little formal training in theory and composition: he put down sounds as he felt they should be heard and disregarded harmonic

[6] Used as the basis for the musical score of the Broadway show *Kismet* in 1953.

[7] When the characters of the Russian alphabet are brought into English phonetically various spellings are possible.

rules in doing so. His output includes a large collection of songs which are of particular interest to vocal recitalists, several operas, some piano music and orchestral works. Three compositions serve as fine examples of his extreme Russian nationalism: (1) the opera *Boris Godunov,* based on a drama by Pushkin; (2) *A Night on Bald Mountain,* which is an orchestral fantasy; and (3) *Pictures at an Exhibition,* which was composed as a suite of piano pieces having as their inspiration a one-man show of the works of the Russian architect and artist Hartmann, but which is more often heard today in one of several orchestral arrangements, the best of which is by Ravel.

The final member of The Russian Five is Nicholai Rimsky-Korsakov (or -Korsakoff) (1844–1908). His early career was as an officer in the Russian navy, and after a tour of duty with the fleet he was made inspector of the navy bands, which gave him an opportunity to become better acquainted with musical instruments. It is perhaps because of this position and the opportunities it afforded him for the study of the instruments and their possibilities that he became the most adept orchestrator of the Russian group, and that he wrote a definitive textbook on the subject of orchestration.

While still in the navy Rimsky-Korsakov had started composing; he was largely self-taught but had enough initiative and desire for musical knowledge to make himself one of the outstanding music teachers of the period. For years he held the professorship of music at the St. Petersburg Conservatory. His best-known music includes the opera *Le Coq d'Or,* from which an orchestral suite is often heard today; the *Scheherazade Suite* based on the tales from the *Arabian Nights,* and used as background music for almost every movie that has an Arabian locale; the *Capriccio Espagnol* for orchestra; and the *Russian Easter Overture,* which is a masterpiece of orchestra color, and which, utilizing pagan music and Orthodox Church themes, was written in memory of Mussorgsky and Borodin.

It should also be mentioned to the credit of Rimsky-Korsakov and as an example of the fine spirit he had in relation to the other members of The Five and Russian music in general that he wrote a considerable amount of music for which he is not given due credit. He completely orchestrated or finished the writing of uncompleted operas by Mussorgsky, Borodin, and lesser-known Russians. A considerably longer life than any of his fellow artists fortunately made possible this labor of love in addition to his teaching and his own compositions.

## *Peter Ilyich Tchaikovsky* (1840–1893)

TCHAIKOVSKY (OR TSCHAIKOWSKY) WAS NOT a member of The Russian Five, but was the greatest of all the Russian composers. He stands also as both the most nationalistic and the least nationalistic of the Russian Romanticists, depending upon which works you may be using as a basis for judgment. Unlike The Five, Tchaikovsky was well trained by European standards in the theory and composition of music, and as a result had a broader aspect of music than his fellow countrymen. So, unless he really tried to be impressively nationalistic, his works do not sound particularly Russian, as for example, much of the music of the *Nutcracker Suite* and many of the tunes that have been popularized in America by the addition of sentimental words. But when he sets out to make the listener think of Russia, he does so in such a wholehearted way, and uses so many melodies from the Church and from folk music, plus the national anthem itself, that a listener cannot help being struck by the nationalism of it all.

Tchaikovsky wrote so much music in so many styles that a listing of all his currently-played compositions would be too lengthy for inclusion here. Some of his major offerings that are well known are the following, under various headings:

Opera: *Eugen Onegin*
Concertos: for violin and for piano
Symphonies: *Nos. 4, 5,* and *6*
Orchestra suites and tone poems: *Capriccio Italien, Marche Slave, 1812 Overture, Romeo and Juliet*
Ballets: *Nutcracker, Swan Lake, Sleeping Beauty*
Quartet: *No. 1 in D major*

Add to this list many fine songs, some piano music, music for string orchestra, and lesser-known works in the fields mentioned above, and you will get some idea of the amount of music written by Tchaikovsky, and his breadth of musical thought.

# The Impressionistic Period

TOWARD the end of the nineteenth century Romanticism had run a long course. Not only had the earlier, strongly musical nations contributed to the world store of great music through composers who excelled in all types of existing music, but many countries new to international recognition had produced one or more composers who took their places among the great. Added to the suite, the symphony, the opera, the oratorio and the Mass, the keyboard music, and the chamber music of the Classical period were the tone poem, the concert overture, the art song, the music-drama, the German romantic opera, the French operatic form, and the ballet. Romanticism had spread music not only geographically throughout the Western world, but had spread it in types of musical expression that were in the public listening domain. Some of the composers had hearkened back to earlier periods, and made use of the polyphonic texture of the Preclassical era or the sonata form of the Classical period; others had disregarded their predecessors and had produced new styles and new musical effects. Melody and harmony, rhythm, timbre, and form were still with us but were put together in new and exciting ways. Romanticism had run a long and productive course.

But in the closing years of the century and during the beginning of the twentieth century more acute changes started to take place. Each fundamental was examined, as it were, and each underwent a rather revolutionary change. With these radical changes in the use of the fundamentals and with the advent of new philosophies concerning the meaning of music and its use, new musical horizons were opened for the contemporary composer.

Of the many new styles of musical composition that have come into being in the past fifty or sixty years only one has become big enough in scope and definite enough in its goals and methods of reaching them, and has lasted long enough as an accepted part of musical literature to be thought of as a distinct school of writing. That is what is known as Impressionism.

As is so often the case, impressionistic music was just one phase of impressionistic art, which actually started with painting, but which showed up in all of the arts. The name itself was originally derogatory, when the French art critics chided the pictures in an exhibition of young and daring artists; one artist had entitled a picture *Impression of a Sunset,* and the critic in question wondered why he could not have painted a sunset rather than his impression of one, since the sunset was so much more obvious. The idea of the impression rather than the object itself stuck, and *Impressionism* it became in music as well as in painting.

Impressionistic music can be examined in two ways: for (1) what it tries to do, and (2) how it does it. The actual aims of impressionistic music are well expressed by the word. The composer does not want either to tell a definite story or to describe a scene in the clear-cut musical colors that the Romanticist would use. He prefers to give a vague impression of that scene, to create a piece of music that will leave to each listener his own interpretation. To do this he changes the normal use of each of the fundamentals in the following ways.

*Timbre* calls for the less-obvious instruments and often the lesser-used extremes of the usual instruments. In orchestra music some of the composers used the *E-flat* clarinet and several members of the saxophone family; they muted the brasses; they emphasized the use of the harp and the celeste. Woodwinds and strings became much more important than brasses and percussions. Even in piano works the extreme ends of the keyboard were often used simultaneously.

*Melody:* The use of the whole-tone scale, discussed in the section on harmony, comes into usage in an overwhelming number of compositions. The scale intervals, being different from those the ear is accustomed to through the music of the previous periods, cause the music to sound strange and different in the melodic line.

*Harmony* also utilizes the notes of the whole-tone scale, giving a different type of chord structure. Chords are also lengthened out in the upper extreme; where a triad (a chord of three tones) or a seventh chord (which includes four notes) were the basis of previous harmony, the ninth chord (consisting of five parts) now comes into common usage.

*Rhythm,* which is one of the most definite characteristics of classical and romantic music, is de-emphasized to create the desired vagueness of sound, by various devices. For instance, the last unaccented beat of one measure is tied over to the first beat of the next measure, so that the normal accent will completely disappear. Or, as soon as a certain meter, such as 3/4, has been established in a few measures, the meter will be changed to a 2/4, and as that begins to creep into the consciousness of the listener it will be changed back again for a few more measures.

*Form* is simply disregarded. What repetitions may occur do so according to no set pattern, and seem to be purely accidental and incidental.

Utilizing any one of these divergencies from standard procedure would suggest a vagueness in that particular part of the music; using all of them simultaneously will create a type of music that will sound completely unlike anything that has been heard previously. And that is just what the impressionistic composers wanted to do, and did.

A good comparison can be made between painting and music, to get at this idea of vagueness. Think of a picture of Westminster Abbey as it might have been painted by a Classical artist. Form would be the important thing: the form of the architecture would be brought out with clarity, and the picture would have been done from that point in the adjoining terrain that would have given the painter the best opportunity to show this form. Now the same thing, painted by a Romanticist: his view would be different, so that he could give emphasis to the water, or to the gardens, or perhaps to the details of a tower or window. It would still be recognizably Westminster Abbey, but certain features would be romanticized. For the third picture it isn't necessary to use our imagination, for Monet, the French Impressionistic artist, painted such a picture. Here we get an impression of Westminster, from across the Thames, painted as if seen fleetingly through one of the lighter London fogs. It is vague rather than definite in delineation; it is the whole rather than some particularly romanticized part; but it is Westminster Abbey and it is beautiful.

The leader in the Impressionistic period was the French composer Claude Debussy (1862–1918). Showing an early interest in music, he was thoroughly and traditionally schooled in piano and theory and composition. Probably one not so well versed could not have accomplished what Debussy did in giving us a new type of music, for he not only used his knowledge of modern harmony and the whole-tone scale to advantage, but often hearkened back to *organum* and the *Greek modes* for subtile effects.

His works are many: the most representative are in the vocal field, with many songs and the opera *Pelléas et Mélisande,* based on the play by Maeterlinck; in piano music, with such pieces as *Clair de lune, Jardins sous la pluie,* and *La Cathédrale engloutie;* in orchestral music, with the prelude *L'Après-midi d'un faune* and the three *Nocturnes* for orchestra: *Nuages, Fêtes,* and *Sirènes.*

A second French composer of stature equal to Debussy's, but a little more recent, was Maurice Ravel (1875–1937). His works are largely for voice, piano, and orchestra. Characteristic compositions include, for orchestra *Pavane pour une infante défunte* and the *Ma Mère l'Oye* ballet (both of which were originally written for piano and later orchestrated), and *La Valse.* The *Bolero,* which is perhaps his best-known orchestral work, is characteristic of Impressionism in only certain ways, for a bolero, being a dance form, demands a definite rhythm, which Ravel has not discarded, and he utilizes one melody with a harmonic basis which is repeated over and over throughout the entire composition. But in the element of timbre the *Bolero* makes an excellent study of impressionistic treatment, for here he requires unusual instruments, and the more ordinary ones he uses in the extremes of their ranges. This is just as fine an example of the impressionistic use of instruments as it is a poor example to study if we are trying to learn to recognize normal instrumental timbre.

While France was the birthplace of Impressionism, its influence was felt on composers of other nations. Among them was Manuel de Falla (1876–1946), who serves as an example of a combination of Impressionism and nationalism. His works reveal his interest in the folk music of his native Spain, yet they are clothed in impressionistic garb. Piano music and orchestral compositions are his best mediums (he also wrote for guitar). His orchestral suite *Nights in the Gardens of Spain* shows both aspects of his music. The works of the Italian composer Ottorino Respighi (1879–1936) were also nationalistic, touched with an impressionistic treatment, particularly *The Fountains of Rome* and *The Pines of Rome,* both for orchestra. England's Frederick Delius (1862–1934) also used the impressionistic approach in his orchestral works, as did the American, Charles Griffes (1884–1920).

CHAPTER 14

# Modern Music

IN DISCUSSING the earlier schools of music it has been possible to present some definite characteristics of each period, but with modern music that is impossible, for modern music, if it refers to the music of the current century, and in particular to the middle of the century, has almost as many offshoots in individual styles as there are composers.

Modernism might be said to stem from new uses of the elements of music itself (as did Impressionism). But in addition there have been numerous innovations and exploratory flights into the realm of sound that characterize the contemporary writings. Many of these have been accepted to some degree; many more have been tried and discarded. Some have their adherents, though the number may be small; most of them have been approached by composers in a completely sincere desire for musical expression in a completely new medium—and some modern writing has perhaps been done with a tongue-in-cheek attitude on the part of the composer with relation to the gullibility of the listening public. Some of the more important aspects of the twentieth century are the following.

*Polytonality* consists of using two or more key signatures simultaneously. For example, a piano composition might have the music for the right hand in the key of two sharps and that for the left hand in the key of four flats. The result is definite dissonance.

*Atonality* goes one step farther than polytonality. It simply disregards any key relationship at all, so that the music has nothing for the ear to use as a basis. There is no key signature, but a liberal sprinkling of sharps and flats occurs throughout. Again dissonance is the result, for if several notes that might normally be used together are employed it might suggest a key, and this must be avoided at all costs.

As if this were not enough of a radical departure, a small (and unsuccessful) group of composers has attempted to divide the usable pitches within the octave into smaller divisions than those represented by the chromatic scale. This type of music is known as *quarter-tone music* and its implications can be seen. On a piano it can be achieved only by having two keyboards, with one tuned a quarter step higher than the other; the stringed instruments and trombones are capable of playing quarter-tone music because of their construction, but all other instruments would have to be rebuilt with very complicated mechanisms, or the performers would have to be able to produce tones halfway between those now obtainable on the instrument by forcing these tones with legitimate fingering but modified embouchures.

Although the foregoing remarks refer primarily to melody writing, they would also have an effect on the harmony of the composition. Chords are used that are constructed on the intervals of the second, fourth, or fifth, as opposed to the construction based on thirds which has been used satisfactorily for the past several hundred years. And even with traditional chord structure several completely different chords may be used simultaneously.

Rhythm is also subject to many changes. This may be done by changing the number of beats within a measure, by using several rhythms at the same time, or by disregarding rhythmic writing entirely by the omission of the measure as a guiding device.

Form, in its traditional sense, also gives way to lack of form. Repetitions may either be haphazard or studiedly nonexistent.

But in the most recent music of this century the treatment of instrumental timbre in unusual and bizarre ways has come to the forefront with the *avant-garde* composers. In Impressionism legitimate instruments were used in a legitimate way—according to traditional performance—but with the extremes of the instruments being emphasized to give a new color to the music. In modern music some instruments are used in a completely new way, and in addition there has been included in the ensembles gathered to perform this music many new "instruments" both electronic and otherwise. One example of traditional instruments being used in a non-traditional way is that of the piano in the hands of Henry Cowell, who, back in the 1920's developed music based on *tone clusters,* which, as the name signifies, represented the playing of a group of contiguous keys on the keyboard by using the fist, or the flat of the hand, or even the forearm for a larger cluster. Any monotony that might accrue to the listener was modified by treating the piano strings as if they were those of a harp, by plucking them. Since then other composers have used (or misused) the piano by other devices: the use of paper or wood or metallic dampers on the strings, beating the strings with mallets, rapping the frame, either inside or out.

The newer "instruments" used to create sound are those in the electronic field. This was a reasonably natural development following the rise of electronics in industry and the application of electronics to sound-producing media. One concert that was given using only electronic devices to produce the sounds was reported by a critic as being "organized and controlled bleats and blurps, whacks and thuds, screeches and screams, rips, whines, snaps, and a whole lot else. . . . amplified by nineteen additional loudspeakers installed at scattered intervals . . ."[1]

Or an electronic background may be given by tape recorder to sounds from other instruments, such as was done with the "other instruments" including parts of various woodwind and brass instruments, a cello and a bass both bowed at the wrong end, and two water buckets.

Possibly as an antidote to this type of concert (although the composers involved would not admit it) the musical rest has received a strong emphasis. This might be seen in listening to *random music* in which there are comparatively short outbursts of sound from one or more members of the ensemble, followed by a period of complete silence, then another outbreak, then more silence, etc. The silences become important: perhaps the ultimate in this particular phase of *avant-gard*ism is a composition by John Cage entitled *4′33″* in which the performer sits at the piano and gazes at a stop watch for four minutes and thirty-three seconds, then closes the piano lid to signify that the composition is ended!

Many of the composers of the twentieth century have experimented in these and other methods of tampering with the established rules of musical art. Others have been content to write in a style that might be termed *Neoclassicism* or *Neoromanticism,* following the trends of earlier musical generations, but with more liberties than were taken by their predecessors. It is too early to judge the lasting values of many of these composers: they may be accepted now by a segment of the public and be completely disregarded a few years hence. Critics are divided in their opinions, and only time will prove the relative importance of much of this new music. For the critics might be wrong, as some

[1] Faubion Bowers in the *Saturday Review* of Nov. 11, 1961.

of them were at any earlier age when they wrote uncomplimentary things about their contemporaries such as Beethoven and Brahms and Chopin and many others at the time they brought their innovations to the listening world.

It is suggested that you decide for yourselves what type of twentieth-century music appeals to you. The following list includes some composers who have done a major part of their work in the present century, but who kept their music on the romantic level, as well as many who can be considered nothing but modernists. Some are dead, many are still living and experimenting. The list is necessarily limited and includes only those represented by at least a few works in the recorded field.

Edward Elgar (1857–1934) was the best of the English composers of the late Romantic school who kept to this style in his twentieth-century offerings. Unfortunately, the "best of the English" is not a very high accolade.

Richard Strauss (1864–1949) has contributed to music literature in symphonic tone poems, opera, and songs. Although he lived and wrote until comparatively recently, his greatest works were written during the last decade of the nineteenth century and the first dozen years of this century. As a result, he should be considered a German Romanticist, even though he introduced innovations in harmony that were considered extremely new and bold at the time. His music is programmatic in the extreme, sometimes objectionably so.

Jean Sibelius (1865–1957) was the great name in the music of Finland where he spent the last years of his life living in semi-retirement on a stipend from a grateful Finnish government. His independent orchestral works are fiercely nationalistic; in addition he was a symphony composer of merit who approached each new work with imagination, and who achieved imaginative results.

The royal family bestowed many honors on Ralph Vaughan

Williams (1872–1958) for his leadership in English music. Originally writing in the folk idiom, he gave a new style to his compositions when past the age of sixty. His choral music and orchestral works are of equal importance.

One of the great names of this century in bringing a completely new aspect to the approach to musical composition was Arnold Schönberg (1874–1951). His purpose was to break away from all established rules and principles; the results are completely atonal. He accomplished this purpose by a division of the scale into what is known as the *twelve-tone* system, in which each chromatic tone within the octave is of equal importance. Melodies contain all twelve tones and these melodies are subject to mathematical variations. Harmony is treated just as shabbily. Whatever we may think of the results, we must admit that Schönberg had the qualifications to invent this new system of composition, for he had been trained in and had produced several fine romantic compositions before his shattering innovation in 1911. His place in music history is one of a keen intellectual who attempted to give music a completely new idea of sound structure and who succeeded to the extent that other modernists have been willing to make use of his ideas in varying degrees, or to present other modifications of the established style.

Two other names in this area, influenced by Schönberg and themselves an influence on younger composers are Anton Webern (1883–1945) and Alban Berg (1885–1935), the latter being responsible for the controversial opera *Wozzeck*. They, like Schönberg, were born in Vienna.

In a chronological listing Charles Ives (1874–1954) is the first American composer to have caused a stir, although admittedly a belated stir, with his approach to composition. The titles of many of his works, particularly orchestral, show the American background.

Ernest Bloch (1880–1959) should be considered a later Romanticist. The task to which he was dedicated was that of giving us music based on the ideas and spirit of the Old Testament. Bloch was a Swiss Jew, but was well known in the United States because of residence here for more than half his lifetime.

The music of Béla Bartók (1881–1945) has had an increasing popularity since his death. Bartók's first major contribution to the field was his successful attempt to bring to public hearing the true native music of his country, Hungary, to offset the romanticized presentations of Liszt and Brahms in their Hungarian rhapsodies and Hungarian dances. He published a considerable amount of music based on Bulgarian and Roumanian as well as Hungarian folk music. His output has been influenced by the Romanticists and the Impressionists, but he ultimately developed a style of his own, which abounds in polytonality and strong rhythmic emphasis. His string quartets, orchestra music, and piano music are particularly important in a study of twentieth-century music.

Zoltán Kodály (1882– ) shares with his countryman Bartók the presentation of the true Hungarian folk themes. His music has remained more Hungarian in feeling than has that of Bartók.

One of the foremost names in the field of modern music is that of Igor Stravinsky (1882– ). A Russian (who became an American citizen in 1945) and a pupil of Rimsky-Korsakov, to whom he owes much, Stravinsky spent much of his time in Paris and more recently in this country. His compositions are numerous and hard to describe, because he uses no set pattern. What is right in his mind for a particular composition is used; as a result there is no set style. Some works are fairly orthodox; others are dissonant and make liberal use of atonality. His style has changed and continues to change with each new work. Particular mention should be made of his ballets, which were subject to considerable criticism when first played in the earlier part of this century, but which are heard now without the slightest raising of an eyebrow. The *Firebird Suite, Petrouchka,* and *Le Sacre du Printemps* are all well-established works in the ballet field.

The career of Edgar Varèse (1885– ) is an interesting one. A Parisian by birth, he came to the United States in 1915 and has remained here. His first works to draw the attention of the *cognoscenti,* with titles such as *Intégrales* and *Ionisation,* the latter scored for thirteen performers on thirty-five percussion instruments, perhaps started the philosophical discussion of modern times relative to music vs. noise. His original place in the musical limelight was followed by some twenty years of contemporary neglect, but as one of the first, and perhaps the greatest experimenter in the potentialities of electronic music he has returned to the forefront in the field of modern music.

The Latin-American composer who has made the greatest impression on music is Heitor Villa-Lobos (1887–1959). This may be due to the abundance of his music as well as its quality. Villa-Lobos was a Brazilian; his works are in almost every medium of musical expression, and many of them show nationalistic tendencies.

One of the most admired and most often heard composers of modern Russia is Sergey Prokofiev (1891–1953). In spite of having to conform to the ideas of musical production required in the Soviet Union he wrote enough music either before the imposition or while in residence elsewhere for his style to become popular with the contemporary listening public. Opera, piano music, and music for orchestra are his chief contributions. Of special interest are his *Peter and the Wolf* for narrator and orchestra, the *Classical Symphony,* which is a modern version of what Haydn or Mozart might have done had they lived in the twentieth century, and the *Lieutenant Kije Suite,* from music written for a motion picture.

French modernism is best represented by Arthur Honegger (1892–1955), Darius Milhaud (1892– ), and Francis Poulenc (1899–1963). All were members of "Les Six," a group organized to promote French music in a manner reminiscent of the Russian Five. Milhaud has influenced American music not only by his writings, but by his many years of teaching in California, particularly at Mills College; in turn, his music has been influenced by the American jazz idiom. Honneger, born of Swiss parentage, showed polytonal structure in melody and harmony; much of his music has been functional for the ballet and the theater. Poulenc, the youngest member of the group gained in popularity through his delightfully witty approach to serious music.

Four other composers who have had a marked influence on the contemporary scene through their teaching positions at American universities are Douglas Moore (1893– ) of Columbia University, most recently in the public eye through his opera *Ballad of Baby Doe;* Walter Piston (1894– ) of Harvard whose *Incredible Flutist* is representative of his instrumental works; Randall Thompson (1899– ) also of Harvard, who has emphasized religious music, such as the *Last Words of David;* and Paul Hindemith (1895– ) formerly at Yale, who moved to this country from his native Germany for the musical opportunities and freedom in composition. Although embracing many phases of Modernism, and being unmistakably a composer of this century, he has happily retained some earlier concepts that make his music more palatable to the average person than is the music of many of his contemporaries.

Other modern composers born before the turn of the century, with representative works include the German Carl Orff (1895– ), *Carmina Burana,* a cantata; Howard Hanson (1896– ), a potent figure in the field of music education through his post at the Eastman School of Music, and a composer of basically romantic symphonic music; Virgil Thomson (1896– ), orchestra music and choral works; Henry Cowell (1897– ), originally noted for his tone clusters; Roy Harris (1898– ), music for ensembles and orchestra, much of it with an American programmatic background.

Born in this century are many composers who have gained recognition, but as birth-dates get nearer the present the names become more controversial than accepted. Some of each group are included for your information.

Brooklyn-born Aaron Copland (1900– ) has contributed much to American music not only through composition but through his desire to explain and educate, by lectures, books, articles, and performances (he has even written music specifically for school groups to perform). His music has a romantic undercurrent, with the influence of both jazz and folk music noticeable. His *Lincoln Portrait* and *Rodeo* are good examples of his compositions.

Born the same year were Alexander Mossolov (1900– ) whose *Iron Foundry* is a good example of "Machine Music," and Kurt Weill (1900–1950), many of whose tunes from works for the musical theater, such as the *Three Penny Opera* have become part of the popular repertoire of this country.

Two Soviet composers, born in the early part of the century, have had their works become well known in America. The Armenian Aram Khachaturian (1903– ) is most popularly recognized for his *Gayne Ballet Suites,* parts of which reached jukebox status. Much more important is Dmitri Shostakovich (1906– ), who has been both the darling and the bad boy of the Soviet government, depending upon whether or not his music was considered bourgeois or representative of the goals of the Sovet Union, by whatever committee might be in charge of such decisions at a stated time. Some of his symphonies, in particular, have been received with acclaim both by the Soviet intelligentsia and the non-Russian "capitalists" alike, in one case because of adherence to the ideals of the Soviets, and in the other case just because they are admirably constructed pieces of interesting music.

For too many years the literature for the concert band depended too much either on transcriptions of works originally scored for orchestra or organ, or on rather inept compositions, many of which were called "overtures" for want of a better name. However, in the recent part of this century many fine composers have written specifically for the band in addition to works for other media of expression. In addition to Aaron Copland, mentioned above, the list includes Paul Creston (1906– ), Morton Gould (1913– ) and Vincent Persichetti (1915– ).

Among other contemporary composers you should know about and watch are several men who have already produced much music of account. These would include the Americans Samuel Barber (1910– ), *Adagio for Strings,* and William Schuman (1910– ), *Credendum;* Gian-Carlo Menotti (1911– ), an American by adoption and a creator of many short operas, such as *The Medium* and the TV opera *Amahl and the Night Visitors;* and Benjamin Britten (1913– ) of England, who seems to have much to say, particularly in the choral field—*The Turn of the Screw* and the recent *War Requiem.*

To round out the list are the following, who might still be considered controversial composers if judged on standards that have withstood the tests of time. John Cage (1912– ), *Amores for Prepared Piano and Percussion;* Ralph Shapey (1921– ), *Evocation for Violin, Piano and Percussion;* Mel Powell (1923– ), formerly a member of the Benny Goodman ensemble and now on the Yale faculty, *Filigree Setting for String Quartet;* Daniel Pinkham (1923– ), *Concert for Celeste and Harpsichord Soli;* and Billy Jim Layton (1924– ), *Quartet in Two Movements.* These are representative of an ever-increasing number of comparatively young musicians who might or might not be recognized and remembered in more than a historical way forty or fifty years from now.

## *THE POPULAR MUSIC OF AMERICA*

Special attention is being given to the popular music of this country because of (1) its popularity with a large segment of the population, and (2) its effect on the more serious music of our time.

America has always had some form of popular music, although in the early days of the country this was not so noticeable because of the European background of our citizens and the presence of their home-country folk songs. The first truly American output of any magnitude came in the middle of the nineteenth century, when the minstrel show was the chief form of public entertainment. It was because of the demand for music for the minstrel show that Stephen Foster (1826–1864) wrote his songs, many of which concerned the southland, and many of which have been accepted into our literature as composed folk songs. Other composers with other equally famous songs also made their contributions at this time, but none was as prolific or as lastingly important as Foster.

As the minstrel show lost favor, it was replaced by a type of entertainment known as vaudeville—a series of acts of one type or another, with no book or continuity. Trained seals, Japanese acrobats, and dramatic sketches were interspersed with popular singers, instrumentalists, and barbershop quartets. Again, here was a medium of entertainment looking for material; the Keith and Orpheum and other vaudeville circuits played in theaters established in many cities, so that a good act might have a long run, and the music used in this act could be heard by many people in many parts of the country. The fact that neither television, nor radio, nor even phonographs were in existence during the early days of vaudeville meant that a new song would not lose its popularity by overproduction in a short time. In fact, it might take a year or two for a new number introduced in New York to reach Washington and St. Louis and Chicago. Sheet music was available, but since repetitions were pretty much up to the ability of someone in the home to play the song on the piano, the songs had a far longer life, and many of them are still popular for informal group singing.

Vaudeville was given a setback by the introduction of the sound track in connection with the motion-picture industry. And again the writers of popular music started to turn out songs for the musical films, which have continued in great demand and have produced some melodies that have achieved nation-wide popularity. At the same time on the legitimate stage there was a rise in the musical comedy and operetta type of production. The music of Victor Herbert (1859–1924), Rudolf Friml (1879–    ), Jerome Kern (1885–1945), Sigmund Romberg (1887–1951), Vincent Youmans (1898–1946), Richard Rodgers (1902–    ), Cole Porter (1893–    ), Irving Berlin (1888–    ), and others became the popular music of the day.

The mechanical reproduction of sound has had both good and bad reactions on the popular music of any given composer. With the advent of the phonograph it was possible for people unable actually to see the shows in New York or on tour to hear the best selections, and to hear them as many times as they desired. With radio, the jukebox, and television it has been almost impossible not to hear the popular tunes. The obvious ill in this system is the fact that (1) it is necessary to put up with a lot of trash that is foisted on the public by so-called composers of popular music, and (2) the constant repetition to which we are subjected will tend to kill off a tune in short order, because it is overworked. The value of mechanical reproduction lies in the fact that a new and good composition is as available anywhere in the country as it is on the West Coast or in New York. If there is any place where discriminating listening is necessary it is in relation to radio and television listening, but unfortunately the average listener will take what comes along with the hope that, even though a program is either mediocre or obnoxious, the one that follows may prove better.

Popular music has not only undergone a series of changes in relation to the possibilities and mediums of production, but it has also changed a lot in style. The ballad type of composition has always remained, and the dance tune has been with us in various ramifications. But the most important phase of change has not been so much with the music itself, but with the music as related to the performing group and the performing style. This is largely concerned with the music for the dance, rather than for voice or for entertainment as such, though a good reproduction of earlier styles will draw an audience of people who are willing and happy to listen to the music without having actually to dance to it.

This whole field of rhythmic dance music is thrown together (incorrectly, to be sure) into what is termed *jazz*. The word *jazz*, itself, did not come into usage until long after the music had come into being, and more recently it has been modified by various adjectives that belie its original connotation. Since the discussion here is to show primarily its impact on more serious and supposedly more lasting music, only a brief outline will be given of some of its more basic subdivisions: hot, straight, modern, and symphonic.

*Hot jazz* can be said to embrace the beginnings of the dance music played by pianists or in small combinations of instruments by the Negroes in New Orleans and the white groups in Chicago that copied the ideas of the Negroes. Memphis and St. Louis and New York and points between all come into the picture with additions and slightly new outlooks, but the art of improvising on a theme (and it was an art) goes back to the Negro bands that played for street parades and for entertaining in some rather unsavory spots in New Orleans. The whole basis of this hot jazz (which certain European writers consider America's most important contribution in the field of original music) is found in (1) a strong underlying and steady rhythm, (2) the imagination of the individual performers, who simply use a given melody as a point of departure for improvisation, and (3) the performer's complete familiarity with, and indeed virtuosity on, his given instrument. Ragtime and barrelhouse, tailgate and blues, the New Orleans style and the Chicago style are merely offshoots of this basic concept. It goes back to the turn of the century and is a Negro invention; it actually did not make much of a dent on our national consciousness until about 1916 when white imitators in northern cities began to perform to an ever-increasing group of interested listeners. It has kept its place, with ups and downs in popularity until the present, and much of the finest in this style can still be heard not only on recordings, but in some of the night spots in New York and elsewhere.

The *straight jazz* is a loose term applied to music that attempted to keep the basic ideas of hot jazz, but to do so with larger instrumental combinations—orchestras of fifteen or more musicians as versus the five- or six-piece "combos" of the earlier style. This necessitated written arrangements, since it was impossible for fifteen men to have the rapport among them that five might have. Within the arranged music opportunity was given to solo instruments to improvise over a background of the rest of the orchestra or parts of it, so that the imagination of individual players was utilized, though not to the degree inherent in the hot style. The imagination of the arranger had to be substituted in the full ensembles to keep away from complete bedlam. *Swing* is the best offshoot of this field, since it more nearly approaches the feeling of the earlier jazz.

A third type seems as different from its predecessors as contemporary serious music is from the compositions of the Romantic era. For want of a better name it can be called *modern jazz,* which at best is a catchall for many channels that have branched off from the main stream of the earlier jazz manifestations. Three of the main categories are (1) *BeBop,* which its originators refuse to concede had anything to do with jazz, but which follows a jazz line to the extent that it can't be considered anywhere else; (2) *cool jazz,* played by a small combination of instruments, with changes in chord structures and with a flowing underlying rhythm; and (3) *progressive jazz,* a name first applied by the orchestra leader Stan Kenton to a type of arranged music performed by large instrumental groups. As jazz musicians have experimented with these styles they have come up with their own variations and performing differences which, in turn, have been analyzed, written about, and publicized by the ever-increasing number of critics who limit themselves to a study of the jazz field. This has brought into the vocabulary of *modern jazz* an ever-enlarging series of categories, such as *West Coast, East Coast, mainstream, hard bop, funky, soul,* and *Third Stream.* To distinguish among these recent arrivals on the scene of performed jazz is something that should be left to the jazz cultists: even the great Duke Ellington admits that the divisions into specific categories are ill-defined and often indefensible.

*Symphonic jazz* is a term applied to the use of some of the more obvious rhythms and harmonies and melodic departures and instrumental usages of jazz applied to the field of more serious music. It is music that is rhythmic, but not monotonously rhythmic; changes take place in the tempo and the meter, and its performance requires working under the baton of a conductor. Three names are linked in the initial production of this type of music with the first performance of the *Rhapsody in Blue,* although other serious composers had previously used some of the jazz idiom in their works. But the *Rhapsody in Blue* started a trend.

The first and most important of these three names is that of George Gershwin (1898–1937). Gershwin was born in Brooklyn, became adept at playing popular music, and broke into the musical headlines by composing first for the Tin Pan Alley publishers and later for Broadway musical comedies, where his name was synonymous with a hit show. As he progressed in composition techniques, he had a brilliant idea. If the dance bands of the day could take music originally written to be played under a conductor's baton, and turn these tunes into dance music (as was being done with *Liebesträume, Song of India, To a Wild Rose,* the *Peer Gynt Suite,* and other familiar melodies), why would it not be possible to do the reverse; to write music that was primarily dance music but that would have to be performed under a conductor as a more serious type of composition? The result was the composition of the famous *Rhapsody in Blue* in 1924. The next phase was to find an opportunity for public performance. Paul Whiteman, who had been the leading large dance orchestra leader for some years, was the answer. He had planned a concert in Aeolian Hall in New York, to be followed by similar concerts of jazz music elsewhere, and the *Rhapsody* filled the requirements of a *pièce de résistance* for his musical presentation. The third name is that of Ferde Grofé (1892–      ), an arranger for Whiteman who was capable of putting Gershwin's ideas on paper (which Gershwin couldn't do at that time). Grofé later produced some good symphonic jazz in his own right, such as the well-known *Grand Canyon Suite.*

Gershwin's genius continued after his *Rhapsody* had been performed. He remained a top writer of Broadway shows, and added many more works in the symphonic jazz field, among which are *American in Paris,* and the *Piano Concerto in F.* His last big contribution before his untimely death was the American folk opera *Porgy and Bess.* Like Mozart and Schubert, who also died at comparatively early ages, Gershwin was very productive, and, like them, he helped to change the path of music, for many composers since his time have seen fit to incorporate ideas from the jazz idiom into their serious works.

# Index